Island Indictments

True crime tales from Galveston's history

Leigh Jones

Galveston Crime Scene Press

Copyright © 2019 by **Leigh Jones**

All rights reserved. No part of this publication may be reproduced, distributed or transmitted in any form or by any means, without prior written permission.

Leigh Jones
Galveston Crime Scene Press
3209 Autumn Court
Pearland, TX 77584

www.galvestoncrimescene.com

Book Layout © 2019 BookDesignTemplates.com

Island Indictments/ Leigh Jones — 1st ed.
ISBN 978-1-7334900-1-6

CONTENTS

Acknowledgements 1
Introduction 3
Dickinson slayer:
The Ellis Lauhon story 5
Love and bootlegged booze don't mix 20
'Unnatural sex act' leads to brutal Bacliff murder 23
From stolen freedom to death row 27
The crime Galveston refused
to forgive 33
'Senile changes' rip a family apart 40
Not a natural mother's act 43
The body in the
Fort San Jacinto bunker 50
Buried alive on the Bolivar Peninsula 53
Seawall attacker guts victim
'like a fish' 57
Shootout shatters Texas City
love triangle 62
Honest, officer, I'm trying
to go straight! 65
Suspicions of incest trigger deadly family feud 70
Discrimination claims and Hollywood defense tactics 74
Sin City, Texas: Easy on gamblers, tough on reporters 78
Stolen whiskey shipment leads to downtown gunfight 80
Headless, disfigured bodies confound island police 84
She shot him because she loved him 87
Two stolen T-shirts nearly cost a police officer his life 90
Murdered over an insult 93
Seaman's murder nearly sparks
Israeli invasion 97
Waiting forever to die 101

Galveston dairy romance sours into midday murder 105

The little girl who beat the
odds—and the tide 112

Teacher's murder prompts death penalty debate 114

About the Author 119

Acknowledgements

This book would not be possible without the hard working journalists at The Galveston County Daily News who have faithfully reported on every aspect of island life since the late 1800s. Nearly all of the material in this book comes from their detailed accounts. The exploits of the rich and famous will always be recorded and preserved for history. But the loves and losses of ordinary people would be lost without local newspapers. Every birth announcement, engagement photo, and obituary helps to weave the tapestry of the community story that makes a place like Galveston unique.

Introduction

This book started as a blog about historic crime on Galveston island and its neighboring mainland communities. Many writers and researchers have chronicled the lives of the island's famous (and infamous) residents. I wanted to tell the stories of people who made headlines for several weeks or months and then faded again into obscurity. Their criminal sagas are more than morbid windows into history. They often sit at the center of cultural issues the community wrestled with. And the outcomes help paint a picture of the attitudes and values that shaped the city over time.

Several of these cases deal with love affairs gone wrong. In addition to assessing guilt or innocence, juries had to grapple with what it meant to be married and what rights each partner had.

Really heinous crimes raised questions of sanity. How could someone of sound mind commit such atrocities? In the first half of the 20th century, jurors seemed more inclined to assume someone was insane if he or she perpetrated terrible violence. But attitudes toward criminals changed as violence became more frequent. Three of the most horrific killers tried on the island in the mid 1950s ended up in mental hospitals. By the 1980s, juries took mere hours to send someone to death row.

My one take-away after three years of researching seven decades of true crime: The good old days never existed. People were just as self-serving and dangerous then as they are today. When it comes to safety and violent crime, we look at the past through the hazy filter of wishful thinking.

All of the stories told here come from the pages of The Galveston Daily News. Some cases contain more detail than others, depending on how much specificity the original reports included. The cases are not presented in any particular order. They are not the worst cases I could find, nor are they the only ones decided in Galveston's long-suffering courtrooms. These are just the cases I discovered during my first layer of research and found interesting enough to write up. No doubt the pages of The Daily News contain many more fascinating criminal histories just waiting to be rediscovered.

CHAPTER ONE

Dickinson slayer: The Ellis Lauhon story

1955

Early on a Saturday morning, Fred Ervidson knocked on the door of the McPherson home in Dickinson, Texas. It was June 25, 1955. Neighbors hadn't seen the family in three days and had started to worry. When no one answered his knock, Ervidson peered through a front window. He saw what looked like someone in bed, so he called the police. Responding officers made a gruesome discovery: Rubye McPherson, her 12-year-old son George, and her 63-year-old mother Zola Norman had been shot to death, apparently as they slept.

The McPhersons—John, Rubye and their sons Jack, 22, and George—had lived in the neighborhood for eight years. Early reports in The Galveston Daily News described the area as quiet and well-to-do. The family was well-liked and well-known. Neighbors described Rubye, a member of the Dickinson Garden Club, as friendly and involved in the community. George played third base for the Red Sox, a local Little League baseball team.

No one could think of any reason someone would want to kill them.

John McPherson worked as a superintendent for Houston-based Edwards Drilling Company. When his family was murdered, he was working on a rig in Sulphur, Louisiana. As investigators combed through his house, looking for clues, McPherson called to talk to his wife, unaware she had been dead for three days. Police broke the news over the phone.

Grief-stricken, McPherson rushed back to Galveston, along with his son, Jack, who had been working with him. But neither could shed any light on what had happened. Investigators dusted for fingerprints and took photos of the house. They found no other signs of violence and no murder weapon. They ruled out motives of robbery or sex, according to the newspaper.

Rubye McPherson's 1953 red and cream Ford sedan appeared to be the only thing missing.

Several days before she was killed, Rubye drove to Sulphur to visit her husband and son. But when she came home on Wednesday, she wasn't alone.

Witnesses told police they saw Rubye at a local restaurant, having a drink with a young man in uniform. She introduced him as a friend of her son's, from the Army. He said he was hitchhiking to California. The waitresses described him as about 6 feet tall and 190 pounds, with brown hair and eyes and a ruddy complexion. They recalled he didn't have much to say for himself.

The mystery man baffled John and Jack, who said he didn't have any Army buddies matching that description. Neither of them saw the man in Sulphur before Rubye left to drive home, leading police to believe she picked him up on the road. Investigators said he apparently ate dinner with the family Wednesday evening. George slept with his grandmother in the guest bedroom that night, leaving the stranger to sleep in his room. A high school friend of Jack's stopped by at about 10 p.m. She was the last person to see the family alive. The coroner said they likely were killed sometime late Wednesday or early Thursday.

On Monday, investigators told a Daily News reporter that John McPherson couldn't find his wife's wedding and engagement rings, worth about $350. The $40 she reportedly had in her purse before she drove home also was missing. And despite launching a nationwide hunt, no other police agencies had found a trace of the missing car.

Police offered an $1,100 reward (worth nearly $10,500 today). But a week after the family's murder, the case had already gone cold.

~ ~ ~ ~ ~

On July 1, 1955, Galveston County lawmen caught a break in the Dickinson triple murder case.

The owner of a used car lot in Nogales, Mexico, became suspicious when an American tried to sell him a red and cream Ford sedan. He alerted local police, who noted the man matched the description of the Dickinson killer and a robber who shot a gas station attendant in El Paso, Texas. Mexican police declared the man an "undesirable alien" and handed him over to American authorities.

It didn't take long to extract a confession. Ellis Euclid Lauhon Jr., 26, admitted to both crimes, and the Texas Rangers flew him back to Galveston to face charges.

During a two-hour interview with Assistant District Attorney Archie Alexander and Sheriff Frank Biaggne, Lauhon described in detail what happened the night of June 22. He admitted he killed Rubye McPherson, her son George, and her mother Zola Norman as they slept. He talked "freely and willingly" about the crime, telling sheriff's deputies a strange tale of lost love and cold-blooded determination.

The headline in the July 5 edition of The Galveston Daily News declared: "'I'm Done For' Says Slayer of Dickinson Trio." Beneath it, the newspaper ran four "candid" jailhouse photos of Lauhon taken by photographer Bill Johnson. They even had him pose reading a copy of the newspaper. Alexander said jailers were taking "special precautions" in guarding Lauhon, but that didn't prevent journalists from gaining easy access to the admitted killer.

Lauhon told deputies he was hitchhiking when McPherson picked him up in Beaumont on her way back from visiting her husband and son in Louisiana. After he got in the car, he pulled a gun, intending to rob her. When she started screaming and told him she didn't have any money, he tried to calm her down by taking the clip out of his .22-caliber pistol and putting it in the car's glove box. He told her he was AWOL from his base in Georgia, and she at first threatened to turn him in. But he claimed she later relented and offered to help him instead, promising to take him home for the night, feed him, and give him money before sending him on his way the next morning.

When they arrived in Dickinson, they stopped at a cafe and had two beers. McPherson introduced him as her son's friend so the restaurant staff wouldn't know he was on the run. When they arrived back at the McPherson home, Lauhon said he ate dinner with the family and then sat in the living room with them, watching television. He stayed up for about two more hours after they went to bed. When he finally turned in, he lay awake for two hours before getting up and taking his pistol from his bag.

He first went into Norman's room, where she was sleeping with her grandson. When she heard Lauhon come into the room, she woke up, and he shot her. When 12-year-old George awoke, Lauhon shot him, too. He told Alexander he planned to knock McPherson unconscious and take her with him so she could write checks along the way to fund his escape. But the club he intended to hit her with slipped from his hand as he swung at her head. When she started awake, he shot her.

Lauhon took $20 from McPherson's purse and slipped the diamond engagement ring and gold wedding band from her finger. He also rummaged around in Norman's purse and scrounged up about $3 and change. Before leaving the house, Lauhon emptied the trash and tried to wipe his fingerprints from anything he might have touched. Then he had a glass of milk in the kitchen and took off in McPherson's car.

Lauhon drove until he reached San Antonio, where he left his service uniform at a cleaners. When he reached El Paso—the day after police discovered his victims' bodies in Dickinson—he stopped to get gas and decided to rob the station. Attendant Edward Highet, 22, told police Lauhon struck him from behind when he turned around to make change after filling the man's gas tank. The two struggled and Lauhon shot Highet in the face. Lauhon made off with about $100. He told the Daily News he thought he'd killed Highet.

If the details of Lauhon's crime spree weren't fantastic enough, his motivation sent it over the top. Lauhon claimed he was trying to get back to Japan, where he'd been stationed starting in 1952. The next year, he fell in love with a young Japanese girl named Taeko and married her in a Shinto ceremony. But her parents would not consent to a marriage on base, and without that U.S. blessing, Lauhon couldn't bring her with him when his deployment ended. When he got orders to return to Eglin Air Force Base in Florida, he told reporters he went back to the apartment he shared with Taeko and slit his wrists. But his wife found him and stopped the bleeding.

After he returned to America, Lauhon was reassigned to Georgia's Robbins Air Force Base in January 1955. He volunteered to go back to Japan but didn't have the qualifications. He told reporters his sergeant advised him to forget Taeko and make the best of his situation. But he was moody and got into fights with the other men. His sergeant threatened to put him in the "stockade" if he didn't settle down. During a half day leave on June 17, he decided to flee the base and make an attempt to get back to Japan.

"Naturally, everybody knew that I wanted to get back to my wife, and the first place they would look for me would be San Francisco, so I decided to fool them all," he told reporters.

Lauhon planned to make it to Mexico or Central America and stow away on a ship headed for Japan. He made it as far as Beaumont, where Rubye McPherson picked him up. Lauhon told reporters the same story he told officials but offered a few more details about how the crime made him feel. He said after he went to bed, he started to get nervous and upset, thinking he would never make it back to Japan. After the murders, he said he was "scared to death."

"It's unbelievable that a man who had never harmed a woman or a child would suddenly turn killer of not one but three persons," he said, describing the memory as like a dream. "I guess I will realize what I have done," he added.

Lauhon, who was from Arkansas, also provided some insight into his family life, saying he didn't have a good relationship with his parents and did not intend to contact them. He said when he brought problems to his parents, his mother always took the other person's side and his father would laugh. He went to the same college his father attended, which the newspaper did not name. But he dropped out after two and a half years. Lauhon said he wasn't a good student and was "nervous from too much study." He worked as a field and farm hand until an Air Force recruiter convinced him to enlist in 1950. But he quickly soured on life in the service, which was nothing like the recruiter claimed it would be, he said.

Daily News reporter Terry MacLeod rounded out her jailhouse interview story by noting Lauhon's faith, or lack thereof. The confessed killer said after making a study of world religions, he had renounced Christianity and no longer believed in the divinity of Christ.

"But nothing matters anymore. I'm done for," Lauhon concluded in a flat tone.

~ ~ ~ ~ ~

Four days after his arrest, Ellis Euclid Lauhon Jr. had an emotional reunion with his father at the Galveston County jail. After that meeting, Ellis Lauhon Sr. sat down with Galveston Daily News reporter Terry MacLeod to talk about his son—and begin to pave the way for his defense.

"I feel the blame is mine," Lauhon Sr. said. "If I knew then what I know now, I would have gone without food and other necessities to provide what my son needed for many years—the help of a psychiatrist."

The father said from his first day of life, Lauhon Jr. was scarred. He was 12 pounds at birth and doctors "mutilated" him with forceps during the delivery. Although he grew and appeared to develop normally, his parents realized he was "deficient in some respects," the father said, describing his son as an introvert.

Mark Woolsey, a family friend and lawyer from Ozark, Arkansas, who traveled with Lauhon Sr. to Galveston, recalled Lauhon Jr. as "peculiar." He said he didn't smoke, drink, or adopt "vices" popular with other boys but seemed obsessed with physical power. Despite that, he did not meet the physical standards for the Air Force, his father said. But he got in based on his high score on the IQ test.

After Lauhon Jr. shipped out to Japan, he wrote his father about his plan to marry Taeko. Lauhon Sr. said he objected to the union, telling his son he would rather he marry someone with a similar background and education. Lauhon Jr. wrote back and told his father he would "divest himself" of the girl. But he didn't, and his sister, Patricia Morton, told their father after his arrest that Lauhon Jr. had written her announcing the marriage. Lauhon Sr. gave the newspaper a photograph of the couple he found in his son's belongings. He also said he found several letters from the girl addressed to "my beloved husband."

But the Japanese teenager at the center of the confessed killer's obsession claimed she never married him. Half way around the world from the drama unfolding in Galveston, Taeko told an Associated Press reporter they were just friends. She also said she was engaged to someone else in Japan and never wanted to see Ellis Lauhon again. Her denials crushed the suspect, who said it was "tragic."

"How I wish she could come to the States and be with me when I need her," he said. "But I don't want to cast any reflections on her."

Although Woolsey said he did not intend to take on Lauhon defense, because of his own commitments in Arkansas, he outlined the future legal team's strategy.

"There is no question in my mind that the boy needs psychiatric care, he is not balanced emotionally," the lawyer said. "All we can do is to present the facts at the trial with no trickery. This is a very regrettable and unfortunate tragedy, which everyone deplores, but this young man is not a criminal. We are not afraid to submit the issue to the courts of Texas."

Three days later, Lauhon Sr. and Woolsey met with well-known Houston lawyer Percy Foreman, who declined to take the case because he had another high-profile case coming to trial at about the same time as Lauhon's. He recommended a Galveston attorney who agreed to mount a defense for a "reasonable fee." But Lauhon Sr. said even that was too much money for the impoverished family. If the Lauhons couldn't raise any money, District Attorney Marsene Johnson Sr. said the state would appoint an attorney.

A grand jury indicted Elis Lauhon on three counts of murder on July 15. Johnson said he would seek the death penalty in the case. He also scoffed at any suggestion of insanity and said he would not move to have a sanity hearing before the trial.

Lauhon Sr. returned to Arkansas to raise money for his son's defense. By mid August, he had hired an attorney—State Rep. Jean Hosey. The judge originally set the trial for October or November, but the district attorney admitted it might be delayed because of the trail of Ann Williams (see Chapter 7). Hosey said he planned to order psychiatric tests for his client as quickly as possible.

At his arraignment hearing on Dec. 6, Lauhon pleaded not guilty.

The trial was set for mid January, but on Jan. 12, Hosey asked for a delay so his client could go to John Sealy Hospital for extensive psychiatric tests that could take up to four weeks. While doctors evaluated Lauhon, Hosey wrangled with Johnson over the confessed killer's diary, found among his belongings after his arrest. Johnson at first refused to turn it over, calling it a key piece of evidence. But on Jan. 20, Judge Donald Markle ordered him to allow Hosey and other members of the defense team to inspect the book.

When the case went to trial in May, it quickly became apparent why Johnson didn't want the diary admitted into evidence.

~ ~ ~ ~ ~

From the moment Ellis Euclid Lauhon's sanity hearing began on Monday, May 14, 1956, witnesses painted for the jury a picture of a deeply troubled man who had suffered from severe mental illness all his life. Family members, childhood friends, his commanding officer in the Air Force, and finally, three University of Texas Medical Branch psychiatrists all testified to Lauhon's instability and inability to tell right from wrong. The volume of evidence pointing to the confessed killer's insanity far outweighed the witnesses calling for him to stand trial for the murder of Rubye McPherson, her 12-year-old son George, and her mother, Zola Norman.

The jury of 10 men and two women—picked over three days from an initial group of 78—had to answer just two questions: Was Lauhon sane on the night he shot his victims while they slept, and was he sane enough to go to trial.

Lauhon's mother, Ruth, recounted her son's traumatic birth and the family's fears it had damaged him irreparably. As a child, she said he had trembling spells and blackouts. One day she came home and found him crouched under his bed, naked and "looking wild." The family doctor had to come give him a sedative to calm him down. She testified the doctor told her he thought her son was a "schizophrenic, paranoid type with catatonic stages." But he never explained what that meant, she said. And though they thought something was wrong with his brain, she and her husband didn't have money for any kind of treatment.

"I just kept hoping Sonny would outgrow his spells and get better," she said. "But he kept getting worse all the time."

Lauhon's sister, 23-year-old Patricia Morton, told jurors she was close to her brother, who never mixed with other boys and suffered teasing at school. She said her brother was "living his life in a novel—a romantic escapade," and his Japanese wife was the first person to play along with him. In letters he sent from Japan, he told her he hated his parents because his father was always putting on a front and his mother never let him grow up. Lauhon told her he was "going to start a one-man war on the United States" because everyone was against him.

Ellis Lauhon Sr. described his son as a bookworm who didn't like sports. That made it hard to connect with the boy as a father should, Lauhon Sr. said. Although kids at school picked on him, he graduated as co-valedictorian of his high school class in Altus, Arkansas. He spent two years at Arkansas Polytechnic College, but his father withdrew him at the request of school officials. Lauhon Sr. didn't find out until after the murders that his son had been stealing from other students to help pay for drugs prescribed to him because he was afraid his sex was changing.

On the second day of the hearing, the defense team read 10 depositions from friends, neighbors, and teachers who knew Lauhon growing up. They all said they thought he was "of unsound mind." Some quotes included: "was most abnormal; obsessed with cleanliness; grew up very antisocial; didn't care to mix with other people; was socially unadjusted." Lauhon's college roommate and childhood friend, Roy Eugene Hatfield, testified that other kids branded Lauhon a "sissie." He said when his friend came back from Japan he was struck by the difference in him.

"He said he was completely shot—could not relax—was completely mixed up," Hatfield said. "He said he felt he had come from one world into another."

Tech. Sgt. Daniel Morris Salter, Lauhon's noncommissioned officer at Robbins Air Force Base in Georgia, told jurors he made six requests to his commanding officer that Lauhon be given a psychiatric examination. Salter said Lauhon had become a Buddhist and was sowing discord among the other men. He believed Lauhon was of subnormal intelligence and unsound mind.

But Dr. Austin Foster, a psychiatrist at UTMB, described Lauhon as "a superior person, above the common herd of mankind, although dangerous to anyone who threatens the tender spots in his personality." Foster also said Lauhon was paranoid and suspicious, struggling to come to terms with realistic situations and lacking common sense. He couldn't understand what motivated other people and suffered from severe delusions.

"In his fantasies, he fancied himself turning himself into a female, and as a fight against this sex changing, he denied it by going into a masculine occupation," Foster said. "He needs constant evidence he is a man."

Lauhon's fantasies split into two contradictory themes: One in which sex was ruled out and women were placed on a pedestal, and the other, which included morbid sexual fantasies of a wild kind, the doctor said. He also said Lauhon scored the highest he'd ever seen on the schizophrenic scale, which means his thinking was broadly disturbed. He testified he did not believe Lauhon knew what he was doing on the night of the murders. Two other UTMB psychiatrists, Dr. Hamilton Ford and Dr. William B. Barnes, also testified to Lauhon's insanity. Ford said paranoid schizophrenia was the most dangerous form of mental illness. Barnes said he thought it very unlikely Lauhon would ever be cured.

The defense team also read from Lauhon's diary, in which he wrote about wanting to kill his commanding officer in Japan and his mother, father, and sister because they could have sex and he could not. He said he wanted to stand on the top of a high mountain and watch an atom bomb destroy America.

Throughout the testimony, Lauhon sat with his chair turned perpendicular to the defense table, looking out a window and showing no expression.

After taking a break on Sunday, the jury returned to the 10th District Court for two more days of testimony. Monday began on a somber note—it would have been George McPherson's 13th birthday.

District Attorney Marsene Johnson first called to the stand the lawmen who arrested Lauhon and brought him back to Galveston. Texas Ranger J.J. Kelvenhagen said he noticed nothing unusual about Lauhon during the 12 or so hours he spent with him. Ranger Eddie

Oliver said he was not qualified to say whether Lauhon was insane but insisted he knew what he had done and knew the difference between right and wrong. He said Lauhon was concerned about his parents finding out. Assistant District Attorney Archie Alexander also testified to Lauhon's normal manner. He said after he typed up Lauhon's confession and gave it to him to read, Lauhon pointed out some spelling errors.

Johnson asked two psychiatrists to evaluate Lauhon. The first, Dr. C.A. Dwyer of Houston, testified Lauhon had "the mind of a cold, cruel, ruthless, heartless killer ... not any different from the usual killer-type criminal ... a very cruel, a very ruthless person. But insane? No."

Dwyer said Lauhon had the abnormal psychopathic personality all killers have. When Dwyer asked Lauhon if he knew there was a law against killing, Lauhon said yes. When Dwyer asked if he should be punished, Lauhon said, "I probably will be." Dwyer said he agreed Lauhon was a paranoid schizophrenic, but "with a little luck and a little less alcohol, I don't believe he would be sitting here today." Questions from the defense about his credentials didn't seem to phase Dwyer a bit.

"I do not profess to be one of the world's best psychiatrists—not even one of the best in Texas—but I do know a crazy man when I see one," he said.

But Johnson's star witness, an assistant professor of neuro-psychiatry at UTMB, stunned the courtroom by testifying he agreed with the defense witnesses who found Lauhon insane. Dr. Irving Cohen described Lauhon as an insecure individual who feels very inferior and inadequate, particularly from a sexual point of view.

"He felt he had a mandate to kill women, and he killed Mrs. McPherson for the good of the public," Cohen said. "He killed her with avowed self-satisfaction he was benefitting the world."

In Cohen's opinion, Lauhon was incurable, dangerous to society, and should be committed to a mental institution.

After deliberating for 4 hours and 20 minutes, the jury agreed.

When the verdict was read, neither the McPherson nor Lauhon families showed much emotion. The confessed killer showed none, leaning back in his chair, staring out the window through dark sunglasses, as though nothing concerned him. But while he waited in the sheriff's office to learn his fate, Lauhon gave one more interview to Galveston Daily News reporter Terry MacLeod.

"I feel right now and I can only explain how I feel at this moment that an invisible hammer is pounding away on my head," he said. "All I want to do is rest for the balance of my life."

~ ~ ~ ~ ~

Ellis Lauhon's story did not end with his sanity trial. Nor did it end with his commitment to an east Texas mental institution, despite promises to the contrary.

On May 23, 1956, the day after the jury handed down its verdict in Lauhon's sanity trial, defense attorney Jean E. Hosey said the confessed killer of three would be committed to the Rusk State Hospital with the recommendation that he be kept there for the duration of his life.

On June 11, two Galveston County sheriff's deputies transferred him to the hospital's maximum security wing. They later told The Galveston Daily News that he talked freely during the 217-mile trip and didn't seem particularly bothered by his circumstances. He said the only thing that troubled him during the trial was the admission of his diary. Hearing his innermost thoughts read aloud in court embarrassed him, he said.

Although he seemed perfectly lucid the day of his transfer, less than three weeks later, his new doctors said he had completely withdrawn from the world.

"Ellis doesn't recognize people and doesn't seem to be cognizant of what is going on about him now," his father, Ellis Lauhon Sr., told Daily News reporter Terry MacLeod on July 26 after trying to visit his son. Doctors refused to allow a meeting.

When contacted by the newspaper, the doctor wouldn't give any information other than to confirm Lauhon was undergoing treatment.

Despite orders that he be committed to the institution for life, rumors of Lauhon's release began to swirl within a few years. On Aug. 19, 1958, the Daily News contacted the hospital to make sure he was still there.

"Anyone familiar with the penal code under which he was committed here would know that neither the district attorney nor the superintendent of the hospital can possibly release this man," said Dr. Charles W. Castner, the hospital superintendent. Castner said in order for Lauhon to be released, the hospital doctors would have to find him sane and then ask the court for permission to release him.

But that seemed unlikely: Castner noted Lauhon's condition had gotten progressively worse in the two years since his commitment.

After that, the man known as the "Dickinson slayer" disappeared from Galveston headlines for 12 years.

In September 1970, the new superintendent of the hospital, Arch Connolly, petitioned 10th District Court Judge Donald Markle, who presided over Lauhon's original trial, for a new sanity hearing. Hospital staff believed Lauhon to be sane, Connolly said. Although he could not be retried for Rubye McPherson's murder, if found sane, he could be tried for killing her 12-year-old son, George, and her mother. But a new trial probably wouldn't produce a different verdict: The murders were committed within minutes of each other, making it impractical for a new jury to find Lauhon sane for two when he'd already been declared insane for the third.

On Sept. 23, 1970, District Attorney Jules Damiani said he would contest any attempt for a new sanity hearing. But Lauhon, now 41, had already been returned to the Galveston County jail in anticipation of a court appearance.

Six months later, a jury of 10 men and two women would again consider his fate. A doctor hired by the defense team testified Lauhon was in remission because of the tranquilizing drugs he was taking. But

Dr. B.W. Henry, county psychiatrist and an assistant professor at UTMB, warned if Lauhon was released back into the public, he would relapse due to the stresses of life outside the hospital. He said Lauhon told him he still had homicidal thoughts and had tried to take his own life in 1968.

On March 22, 1971, after deliberating for 22 hours and 45 minutes, the jury decided Lauhon needed to be confined for his own protection and that of others.

So back to Rusk he went—but not for long.

Two years after Lauhon's second sanity hearing, Markle agreed to allow Lauhon to be transferred to the Veterans Administration Hospital in North Little Rock, Arkansas, to be closer to his family.

A month later, on May 7, 1973, Lauhon walked out the hospital doors a free man.

Galveston officials did not find out about his release for a year. Markle insisted Lauhon had gained his freedom illegally and that only a jury could declare him sane and free to leave the hospital. According to the Daily News, Markle was preparing an order to have Lauhon brought back to the island.

That was the last time Lauhon made headlines in Galveston.

After 17 years in a mental institution, Ellis Lauhon, spent the next 40 years living an evidently quiet life in Hot Springs, Arkansas. He died on Jan. 25, 2013. He was 83 years old. His short obituary in the Fort Smith, Arkansas, Times Record made no mention of the McPherson family or his time in Texas.

"He spent his life seeking to further his knowledge of a variety of subjects," the obituary claimed. "He was an avid reader. He also loved music and movies."

CHAPTER TWO

Love and bootlegged booze don't mix

1930

Spectators packed into the 56th District courtroom on Nov. 14, 1930, for a sensational murder trial. By the time J.W. Coward, the second witness for the defense, took the stand, a blue haze of cigarette and cigar smoke filled the room.

Coward told the jury that John W. Adams "worshipped the very ground that Marie Doherty walked on." For her part, Marie said several times she "would rather die than give him up," Coward recalled.

The crowd gasped in unison over the bold declaration. Doherty, a 27-year-old divorcée, was half her lover's age. Adams was a well-known island official who'd also served as a former deputy sheriff and probation officer. At the time of the trial the white-haired, red-faced man held the position of special officer of the Galveston, Houston & Henderson railway.

He didn't deny shooting Doherty. But he claimed it was an accident sparked by her obsession with him. Prosecutors maintained Adams killed Doherty in cold blood after the passion of their tawdry affair cooled.

As the early spring sky faded toward dusk on March 6, 1930, Adams came looking for Doherty at her house at 215 16th Street. He didn't find her, but he did discover a jug of whiskey under the kitchen table. After pouring himself a half tumbler, he took his gun and marched across the street to a well-known, if seedy, speakeasy.

One of the later witnesses described Ernest Sigmon's establishment as "just an ordinary rat beer joint." Adams banged on the door and asked for Marie. The proprietor said she wasn't there and told Adams to go away. But he forced his way through the door, firing one shot into the floor. Adams stalked through every room in the house, firing three more shots into the floor. He eventually found Marie hiding behind a door.

Witnesses gave differing accounts of what happened after that. Some said Adams dragged his young lover down the steps and across the street, holding her arm with one hand and pointing the gun into her side. Others, including Adams, said they left together amicably. At one point, he stumbled and she helped him up. When they got to her front porch, one witness said they appeared to be arguing with Marie trying to pull away as Adams continued to point the gun at her. Adams claimed Marie tried to grab the gun from him, vowing to end her own life rather than give him up.

When the gun went off, the bullet tore through the young woman's abdomen and skittered down the hall. She collapsed, a pool of blood quickly spreading beneath her. Adams went to a neighbor's house to call for help but no one would come to the door. He ended up walking to the corner store owned by A. Del Pappa and summoned the police and an ambulance. When Marie arrived at John Sealy Hospital, she confirmed to police that Adams shot her, but couldn't say much else. A few hours later, she died.

When he took the stand on the second day of his murder trial, Adam denied Coward's claim he "worshipped" Marie. He said he fell into her clutches during a weak moment when his wife was ill. He described Marie as "unruly," especially when she'd been drinking. That's why he went to get her from Sigmon's place that day, he said.

"She would come down to where I was working and get into my car and I couldn't get her out," he said. "I tried several times to break away, and I told her finally that if I didn't break away, I'd lose my wife and my job and everything I had in the world, and she threatened to kill me and my wife and herself if I did."

Coward and other witnesses bolstered that claim by recounting a time when Marie had to be taken to the hospital after trying to poison herself. Coward said he heard Marie make threats against her rival.

Adams' wife, Grace, sat through the trial at her husband's side, excusing herself only during the testimony about his devotion to Marie. She had already suffered through a terrible battle with breast cancer, the illness that evidently drove Adams into Marie Doherty's arms. Just before he was scheduled to stand trial in May, Grace took a turn for the worse and prosecutors agreed to put the trial on hold until the end of the year. Although she initially was described as a material witness for her husband, The Galveston Daily News never mentioned her taking the stand.

Prosecutors asked jurors to impose the death penalty. As part of their defense strategy, Adams' lawyers described to the court—in vivid detail—what happens to someone in the electric chair. Adams and his wife sobbed so loudly during the closing arguments the judge had to warn them to settle down.

After two and a half days of testimony, jurors debated Adams' fate for three hours and 45 minutes.

When the foreman read the verdict of "not guilty," Adams collapsed again in tears, then rushed to the jury box to shake each man's hand. After that, Adams faded from the news—mostly. In March 1931, he was back in court again, this time before the justice of the peace, after another woman filed charges against him for cursing and abusing her. The newspaper never reported whether he was found guilty.

It's not clear what happened to Adams after that. His wife died in 1936, and he was listed as a survivor. But after that, The Daily News never mentioned him again.

CHAPTER THREE

'Unnatural sex act' leads to brutal Bacliff murder

1967

Ollie Quinn's phone rang at 2:53 a.m., jolting the Dickinson assistant fire marshal awake.

> *"Please hurry... I need help... my mother is dead. This is Carl Harris."*
>
> *"Can I help you with first aid?"* Quinn asked, now very much awake.
>
> *"No. Her throat is cut. She's dead. I'm at 4427 in Bacliff."*

Quinn tried to get the street name, but the caller had already hung up. He quickly called the Galveston County Sheriff's Office to relay the information, then turned on his police scanner to follow their progress.

At 3:06 a.m. the phone rang again.

"Please hurry.... I need help. Now her girlfriend is dead. I'm at 4427 19th Street in Bacliff."

Quinn, who got any call made overnight to the Dickinson fire house, relayed the information to the sheriff's office and waited. A few minutes later, Deputy Constable Jack Carter and his wife arrived at the grisly scene. They found Mrs. William D. Morwood and Mrs. Martha E. Beene laying in bed, blood pooled around them. The killer had beaten them around the head and face and then slashed their throats.

Deputy Sheriff Warren Lemmon arrived a few minutes later. He found 20-year-old Carl Bruce Harris, Morwood's foster son, in the front yard.

"Oh my God, Mr. Lemmon," Harris said. "Ain't this terrible? To think that anybody would do this for a stinking $5 or $6."

It was Jan. 15, 1967. Although $6 would amount to about $42 today, that still seemed like a pittance for murder. They found bloody fingerprints and no money in Morwood's purse, but Beene's bag still contained $45—about $340 today.

Investigators immediately questioned Harris' story. The home showed no signs of forced entry, and someone had taken the time to wash the murder weapon—a 5 inch kitchen knife. They also discovered bloody footprints in the bedroom and adjoining living room.

Harris, who had lived with the Morwoods since he was 18 months old, had a long criminal record. He was serving a five-year probated sentence for burglary at the time of the murders. Harris later said he knew they suspected him when sheriff's department investigator Fred Greiger arrived at the house. Still, Harris protested his innocence.

"You gotta find out who killed my mother and Martha!" he insisted.

Greiger took him to the Texas City Police Department for questioning. In his pocket, they found seven blood-stained $1 bills. When he took his shoes off, they found blood between the toes of his left foot.

Harris eventually confessed.

Prosecutors charged him with two counts of murder.

Harris went on trial for his mother's murder eight months later, represented by two public defenders from Texas City. His signed confession, read several days into the trial, caused quite a stir. In it, Harris claimed he killed the women because he caught them in "an unnatural sex act" after walking through the home's unlocked front door. He claimed the women immediately started yelling for him to leave.

"I was in the bedroom," Harris said in his statement. "I pushed Martha, swung at Mother—that's when the blood first started. I got scared, both hollered at the same time. I hit Martha and then I hit Mother—knocked them unconscious. I ran to the kitchen, grabbed a paring knife. I don't remember which I cut first. I didn't realize I had cut them until I saw the knife in my hand."

Harris's attorneys objected to the admission of the confession, saying deputies hadn't adequately advised him of his rights before he gave the statement. Prosecutors disputed that claim and the judge ruled Harris knew his rights.

Dr. James Markette, an assistant professor of psychiatry and neurology at the University of Texas Medical Branch, offered the most insight into Harris' motivation. He described Harris as a "sociopathic personality of the antisocial type." He blamed the condition, which he called a personality disorder, on Harris' inability to develop constructive relationships with adults during his childhood. Based on Harris' descriptions of his youth, Markette concluded he suffered from a "gross lack of parental love." But his parents had told him plenty about homosexuality, describing it as "sinful and disgusting." When he caught his mother doing something she had so vehemently opposed, he snapped, Markette concluded.

In their closing arguments, prosecutors disputed Harris's description of his mother's relationship with her friend, noting he could easily have repositioned the bodies after he killed the women to make it look like they were in bed together. They suggested robbery could have been Harris' motive, even though he hadn't touched the money in Beene's purse.

Although Markette blamed the Morwoods for Harris's condition, he did not absolve the confessed killer. He knew what he was doing, Markette said, and understood the consequences of his actions: "Such a person has a defect of conscience. He will act on whim, is always in conflict with others, and can't learn from past mistakes. ... Prisons are full of such people."

And Harris would soon be one of them. On Sept. 25, 1967, the jury took an hour and 45 minutes to find Harris guilty of murder. Jurors concluded even more quickly that he deserved the ultimate punishment—death.

But Harris' story did not end there.

CHAPTER FOUR

From stolen freedom to death row

1969

At about 3:30 a.m. on Friday, Nov. 21, 1969, Deputy Tony Socias Jr. was making his rounds at the Galveston County Jail. When he reached the third floor, he noticed water filling the hallway. He rushed to cell 3G, where the flood appeared to be seeping under the bars. In the middle of the cell, he saw prisoner William Smith "Butch" Ainsworth facedown on the floor, with his cellmate, Joseph McMahon, standing over him.

"Butch is hurt, and hurt bad," McMahon told the deputy. "We couldn't get the water stopped."

Socias pulled out his keys and unlocked the cell door. As the deadbolt scraped out of the lock, the unsuspecting jailer unleashed what The Galveston Daily News described as a "reign of terror" that would captivate Galveston County for two days and take more than 100 lawmen to subdue.

When Socias stepped into the cell, McMahon slammed him into the bars while Ainsworth leapt up and started to choke him. Once they had Socias under control, the prisoners ordered him to call the night jail sergeant to come help with the water. If he refused, they said they would choke him to death.

After Socias made the call, McMahon, a robbery suspect, and Ainsworth, a murder suspect, took his keys and locked him in their cell. Then they freed Carl Bruce "Buster" Harris, a convicted murderer. When Sgt. Ernest Tudor arrived to check on the water, the prisoners beat him to the floor and stole his pocket knife. They forced Tudor to go to cell 3D, which held six prisoners. The escapees ordered him to release just one—Ronnie Roper, who was being held for the same murder as Ainsworth. At cell 3F, they freed armed robbery suspect George Earl Howard, completing their crew.

With the two deputies in tow, the five prisoners made their way to a hallway monitored by closed circuit television. Socias unplugged the camera, knocking out the feed in the control room on the first floor. The group waited five minutes for dispatcher Frank Oakley to call Tudor for a safety check. With Ainsworth holding the pocket knife to his throat, Tudor assured Oakley everything was fine.

The prisoners loaded their two hostages onto the elevator and went to the first floor, where they needed to gain access to the locked control room to open the three doors leading to freedom. Socias went to the control room and Oakley opened the door. After the deputy stepped inside, Ainsworth bolted toward the opening. But out of the corner of his eye, Oakley saw the prisoner coming and tried to slam the heavy metal door. Ainsworth got his arm in the doorway just in time to stop it closing, but it crashed down on his hand. Tudor jumped on Ainsworth but couldn't subdue him, or prevent him from pulling the knife and putting it to Oakley's throat. The injured prisoner ordered the dispatcher to open the doors.

Roper took a .38-caliber pistol from the jailers' storage locker and gave it to Ainsworth, who held the deputies at gunpoint while his fellow escapees looted the personal effects of the other prisoners, netting about $200. Howard took the escapees' files from the booking office. Before walking out of the jail, the five men locked the jailers in a padded cell and demanded Tudor hand over his car keys. Hoping to slow them down, he gave them the key to the trunk, not the ignition.

In the parking lot, while the prisoners were loading into Turdor's car, Deputy Bob Williamson arrived for work. They pounced on him, taking his gun and holding him hostage. As they were trying to get Tudor's car to start with the trunk key, a passerby stopped to help.

Edward Muller was on his way home from taking his wife to work at the University of Texas Medical Branch. That was just the beginning of a very bad day for the retired electrician.

With Ainsworth in the lead, the prisoners piled into Muller's car, dragging him and Williamson with them. They peeled out of the jail parking lot shortly before 5 a.m.

~ ~ ~ ~ ~

Ringleader Butch Ainsworth, who was awaiting trial on a murder charge, wanted to go to Hitchcock, where he said they could get another car. But George Earl Howard convinced them to go to his parents' house in Texas City. When Howard's father refused to give them his car, Ainsworth pulled a gun on him and the fugitives took it anyway.

Howard stayed behind. He hung around long enough to change clothes, leaving his parents' house shortly before deputies arrived to question them. The officers urged the Howards to persuade their son to give himself up. Not long after that, at about 9 a.m., Howard's mother called Texas City police and said her son had returned and was ready to surrender.

Meanwhile, the rest of the fugitives—Ainsworth, Ronnie Roper, Joseph McMahon, and Buster Harris—hadn't gotten very far. The car ran out of gas after only four blocks. The men spotted another car in a nearby driveway and broke into the house, where they found Irene Alexander and her 12-year-old son, Tommy. Taking them hostage as well, the fugitives loaded into the Alexander family car and continued to head inland.

By this time, police from all over the state swarmed the county looking for the escapees. They set up blockades on all roads leaving Galveston county. Search teams included Texas Rangers and Department of Public Safety officers. A Houston Police Department helicopter scoured the bayshore area and the swamplands around Hitchcock. Tips and suspected sightings came flooding in.

But the escapees managed to make it to Dickinson undetected. There they broke into the Nicholls home, where they holed up for the next 17 hours, adding Robert Nicholls, his wife, and his mother to the four hostages they already had.

"They were real nice to all the women," Mrs. Nicholls later told police. Once or twice they spoke angrily to her, "but they were almost always respectful to us."

The men didn't fare so well. The fugitives severely beat both Galveston Sheriff's Deputy Bob Williamson and Edward Muller, threatening at one point to "blow their heads off" if they moved.

For most of the day Friday, the fugitives drank whiskey and watched television reports of the effort to recapture them. The tension—and maybe the alcohol—soon fractured the crew. Ainsworth and McMahon had started to argue by the time the men fled the Nicholls home sometime after dark, Muller later told police. They left behind Muller, Nicholls, and his mother.

By midnight, the fugitives had made it as far as Richmond, where the tension between them exploded in gunfire. Joseph McMahon caught a bullet in the neck.

"We checked his pulse and heart," Harris later told police. "He must have died instantly, so we dumped him out."

Not long after dumping McMahon, they shot Williams too—one bullet lodged in his back and one grazed his head. Thinking they'd killed him, they rolled Williams out of the car. But after they drove off, the deputy got up and managed to walk to Richmond, where he flagged down a passing motorist. He eventually led police to McMahon's body.

Despite the roadblocks and intense manhunt, the fugitives escaped Galveston County and got almost to La Grange before they stopped again. Taking one of the female hostages with them, two of the fugitives knocked on the door of the Heger home at about 3:30 a.m. They said they were looking for a family who lived in the area and asked to borrow a phone book. When Anna Heger opened the door to hand it to them, one of the men grabbed her arm and pushed their way inside the house. The fugitives tied up Heger and her mother in the back room while they raided the kitchen and bathroom for supplies. They took canned goods, bread, medicine, deodorant, and mosquito repellant. They also took two rifles and two shotguns.

"This is it," Heger recalled the fugitives saying after they found the guns. "We got what we came after."

Before they left, they cut the phone line and some electrical wires on the Hegers' car. The women quickly escaped after they heard the fugitives drive off. But Heger had to walk for a quarter of a mile before she could hitch a ride into town to call the sheriff from an all-night service station.

"I've seen it happen on TV, but I didn't ever think it would happen to me," she said after the ordeal was over.

~ ~ ~ ~ ~

Butch Ainsworth, Ronnie Roper, and Buster Harris hoped to get as far as Mexico. But they only made it to Flatonia, Texas.

In the early morning hours of Nov. 22, the fugitives stopped to get gas at a service station in Schulenburg. After they drove away, with their three hostages, the attendant called police. Another witness spotted the group headed into the woods near Flatonia later that morning.

Officers from several law enforcement agencies converged on the area. A deputy sheriff spotted their abandoned car, and a helicopter flying overhead saw a woman waving from a clearing in the trees. One of the fugitives fired at the chopper, but the men eventually decided it was futile to try to shoot their way out. They were surrounded, outmanned, and outgunned.

After signaling they wanted to surrender, the fugitives each took a hostage as a human shield and walked out of the woods.

"I'm just going to try and forget it now," Mrs. Robert Nicholls said after she was freed.

The other hostage, Irene Alexander, cried during an interview with reporters. Her 12-year-old son, Tommy, said he was ready to go back to school. The day he spent as a hostage was his first time to miss class in two and a half years, his mother said.

Galveston deputies returned Harris, Roper, and Ainsworth to the county jail and held them under maximum security until they went to trial.

George Howard, who surrendered just a few hours after the escape, was the first to face a jury, in May 1970. During testimony in that case, Roper described Ainsworth as the enforcer and said the other men were too afraid not to go with him when he hatched the breakout plan. Roper also fingered Ainsworth as the triggerman in Joseph McMahon's shooting. When he took the stand in his own defense, Howard testified he feared for his life. Even so, the jury gave him five years in prison. He got off lightly, compared to the other three escapees.

In 1971, Roper got 15 years in jail.

Days before he would have gone on trial in 1972, Ainsworth pleaded guilty to assault with intent to commit murder for shooting Sheriff's Deputy Bob Williams. The judge sentenced him to 30 years in prison.

Carl Bruce "Buster" Harris ended up with the harshest sentence—death. But he spent less than two years on death row in Huntsville. In June 1972, the U.S. Supreme Court overturned 39 death sentences, including Harris's. The court said jurors who opposed the death penalty were illegally excluded from the panel that considered Harris's case. Galveston County District Attorney Jules Damiani at first said he would seek a new trial. But in August 1972, Texas Gov. Preston Smith commuted Harris's sentence to life in prison. The Texas Court of Criminal Appeals confirmed the sentence in September.

Harris eventually won parole and died in 1993. He was just 46 years old.

CHAPTER FIVE

The crime Galveston refused to forgive

1938

Galvestonians have always taken pride in their tolerance, especially during the years when they called their home "The Free State of Galveston." For decades, the island's well-known underworld dons flouted state bans on gambling, prostitution, and just about all other kinds of illegal vice. Islanders—including law-enforcement officials—overlooked most of the bad behavior with a wink and a nod. But at the end of 1938, one of Galveston's shady characters took one too many steps into the light, revealing an ugliness the rest of the community could no longer ignore.

Calls to clean up the lawlessness lasted for a few years—long enough to make sure the scapegoat paid the ultimate price for everyone's sin. But the demand for virtue soon dissipated, softened by the mellow sea breeze and Galveston's laissez-faire entropy.

In the early hours of Christmas Day 1938, Harry Phillips and Winifred Woodier were celebrating their engagement with two friends at Deppen's bar, a popular beachfront hangout at the corner of 37th Street and Seawall Boulevard. Not long after midnight, Phillips took Woodier back to Rebecca Sealy nurse's quarters. He returned to the bar just long enough to ask his friends, John Miranda and Paula Sharp, if they were ready to go. As Phillips half sat, half leaned on a stool next to Sharp, a man in a dark suit walked up and tapped him on the shoulder.

"Hey buddy, do you mind? That's my stool," said the man, later identified as Leo Lera, a thug working for the Maceos.

According to Sharp, Phillips apologized and started to stand up when Lera punched him in the face. When Miranda tried to intervene in the ensuing scuffle, Lera's friend Mike Calandra, also a Maceo enforcer, pinned him against a wall. Four shots echoed through the small space. Phillips crumpled to the floor.

Miranda carried his friend to the car and rushed him to John Sealy Hospital. Doctors pronounced him dead a few hours later. The fatal shot entered just below his left ear and exited from the top of his head, giving him zero chance of survival. Lera and Calandra turned themselves in to police the next morning, but it's likely they didn't expect to be behind bars long.

Police Chief Tony Messina, along with Miranda, Sharp, and Woodier all said they received threats and warnings to drop the charges. "You keep quiet. Maybe you'll be run out of town," read a postcard addressed to the chief.

The threats might have worked had outrage over the murder and the universal cry for justice not reverberated so loudly. Messina did eventually get run out of office but only because islanders viewed him as complicit with the city's out-of-control lawlessness. Phillips's murder, simply for sitting on the wrong bar stool, created a community-wide uproar. Threats of mob violence against the jailed gangsters prompted the Texas Rangers to offer assistance, which an indignant Sheriff Frank Biaggne refused. Instead, he increased his stock of tear gas bombs at the jail and put his two infamous prisoners under extra guard.

Phillips, 24, worked as the assistant chief engineer, under his father the chief engineer, at Galveston Ice and Cold Storage Co. He had no ties to the organized crime woven through so much of Galveston society. Later accounts of the murder and the subsequent trials described him as a "well-known Galvestonian." Attempts during the trial to paint him as the aggressor fell flat. So did Lera's attempt to claim the derworld. During closing arguments, Johnson urged jurors not to punish his client for the island's political climate.

"Don't send this boy up because of some myth as to any conditions—any political conditions—that may exist in this city," he said. "Be sure, gentlemen, be sure, before you agree on anything like death."

Much of the emotion and tension surrounding the first trial had dissipated by this time, according to The Galveston Daily News reporter covering the proceedings. Although curious spectators packed the courtroom as before, the "general atmosphere" was "noticeably different," lacking the embittered hostility over Phillips's death. When the jurors lingered over their decision, spectators began whispering about a possible hung jury. Judge Charles Dibrell sequestered the 12 men overnight in the courthouse. By the time they were ready to deliver their verdict the next morning, most of the crowd had gone home. Leo Lera stood at the front of an almost empty courtroom to hear the jury pass its judgement.

Verdict: guilty. Punishment: death.

Johnson appealed immediately. Dibrell overruled his motion for a new trial, and the attorney again took his case to the Texas Court of Criminal Appeals. As it had before, the court in Austin ordered a new trial, giving Lera another chance to save his life. This time, Dibrell agreed to move Lera's trial out of Galveston, to Richmond in Fort Bend County. The testimony took only one day—Nov. 8, 1941.

The island's reputation for coddling crime again featured prominently, almost serving as a silent witness for the prosecution. During the closing arguments, Richmond mayor C.L. Dutton, who assisted Johnson in Lera's defense, noted the trial included so much discussion about gambling and drinking that "it must be one of the big businesses of Galveston." He then turned to the prosecutors and asked them why they didn't clean up their city.

That bit of courtroom showmanship played right into Assistant County Attorney Emmett Magee's hands.

"Gentlemen, give us a chance and we'll enforce the law in Galveston," he said during his closing argument. "Give us a chance by convicting this defendant, and we'll take care of lesser matters in Galveston."

Although the 12 men, mostly farmers, who debated Lera's fate for a third time had no vested interest in sending a message to Galveston's criminal underworld, they seemed even less likely than islanders to excuse such a serious crime. They took less than five hours to reach a conclusion.

Verdict: guilty. Punishment: death.

According to The Daily News, Lera showed little emotion as the court clerk read the verdict. Perhaps he thought he would get yet another chance. Johnson immediately appealed the verdict, and Lera went back to the Galveston County Jail for another year while the appeal process played out. But this time, Johnson could not convince the Court of Criminal Appeals to overturn the judgment.

On Nov. 9, 1942, Lera returned to Richmond for his formal sentencing. Spectators again filled the courtroom, and a tense silence filled the air when the judge offered the condemned man a chance to speak.

"In spite of me being found guilty by three juries, I am innocent as far as taking that boy's life with malice aforethought," he said, laboring under intense emotion. "It was an accident. There was so much public interest in the case due to the fact that I was on one side of the fence and that boy was on the other. My reputation and the reputation of some of my people was the reason I was given the death penalty. ... If God doesn't spare me one way, he will spare me another. I want to say something I never thought I would say. I have accepted the Lord Jesus Christ as my Savior, and he has saved me."

The group of Galveston pastors and lay ministers who provided church services inside the jail began a petition drive to ask for clemency for Lera. They called him a changed man, and credited him with helping change the lives of several other inmates. If freed, he could continue that work in the community, they argued. Johnson also continued his efforts in Austin to have his client spared the electric chair.

But Lera's fate was sealed.

On Feb. 20, 1943, the state of Texas executed Leo Lera at Huntsville. The Daily News reporter who witnessed Lera's death provided a gut-wrenching account for the next day's paper. "Lera was pale, distraught, and quietly calm," appearing "dazed and apparently resigned to his fate," as the guards led him into the chamber. When given a chance to say a few last words, Lera thanked the people who had been nice to him and who had helped him with his trial. Then he turned to the small crowd of about 25 spectators.

"God bless each and every one of you," he said before the guards strapped him into the chair.

CHAPTER SIX

'Senile changes' rip a family apart

1955

Nine-year-old Frances Jean Wallace sat happily sharpening her crayons, singing along to the radio, in her parents' Texas City home on a warm afternoon in August 1955. Her grandfather was trying to take a nap in the other room, but the little girl's childish noise chased away his coveted slumber.

Robert Wallace, 78, later recalled getting up and going into the kitchen to get a glass of milk. Instead, he suddenly seized a hammer and walked over to Frances Jean, who evidently didn't see him coming. He hit her once in the center of the forehead, presumably knocking her unconscious. After pulling her chair away from the table, Wallace continued to bludgeon the little girl, hitting her about 20 times until her broken body crumpled to the floor. Then he took the hammer back to the kitchen and sat down near the body, waiting for the little girl's older sister to come home.

When 13-year-old Glenda Fay returned from playing with friends and saw her sister lying on the floor, she ran screaming to a neighbor's house. The neighbor rushed over and, aghast, asked Wallace what happened. He simply told her he'd killed his granddaughter because she was making too much noise.

The gruesome scene horrified the police officers and ambulance attendants who responded to the neighbor's call for help. Texas City Police Chief O.C. Beard described it as "the most gruesome experience in all his years on the police force." Wallace was booked into the

Galveston County jail. Frances Jean's parents, who were at work at the time of the murder, were admitted to the hospital to be treated for shock.

The Wallace case traumatized the county and led to community soul-searching over care for the elderly, a hot topic nationwide. County officials considered the situation especially dire in Galveston, where no "home for the aged" existed at the time. In a story about the state of the elderly, written by Galveston Daily News reporter Terry MacLeod, Probate Judge Hugh Gibson said the problem of caring for the elderly was acute but hadn't been exposed sufficiently. Many families came to him for advice on how to care for their parents, who often struggled with health and mental issues and presented a danger to their loved ones, he said. Gibson lamented the community was not meeting its obligation to care for those who paved the way for current generations.

"If we regarded the human being as a machine, when it becomes old it could be scrapped," he said. "But the human being has a soul, and consequently is entitled to the dignity of man, whether he be 15 or 100."

According to family members, Wallace had been suffering from depression and the effects of what doctors called "senile changes" for a while. Some of the family wanted him committed to a mental hospital, but not everyone would agree to it. Frances Jean's parents had warned her and her sister to run if their grandfather started acting strangely. But up to that point, he'd only tried to harm himself, attempting suicide several times in the months preceding the murder. Family members said he loved the little girls, a claim he repeated to MacLeod when she visited him later in the hospital. He said he didn't know what came over him, and several months later didn't seem to understand what he had done.

Mourners packed Frances Jean's funeral. "From out of great sorrow can come good, if people permit it," said the Rev. Finis Williams, pastor of First Baptist Church. That evening, at the family's home,

MacLeod approached the devastated parents, Glenn and Thelma, who had retreated to their bedroom. Glenn had taken a sedative but could not sleep. His wife perched on the edge of the bed, biting her trembling lip to keep from bursting into tears.

"He has two big hurts, and he can't talk about them now," she said of her husband. "Maybe later, maybe never."

After that, Daily News coverage of the case tapered off. The paper noted a scheduled sanity hearing for Wallace on Jan. 16, 1956, but never reported the outcome. However, his obituary appeared in the paper on Feb. 13, 1957, noting his place of death as Rusk, Texas, home to the state's mental hospital.

While the memory of Wallace's horrific crime might have faded, the need it exposed did not. Five months after the Wallace murder, the Moody Foundation announced plans for a retirement home, the county's first. Such a facility had long been a dream of W.L. Moody Jr., according to his daughter, Mary Moody Northen. But it would take another six years before the home became a reality.

In July 1958, the foundation bought 31 acres from the federal government's sale of the Fort Crockett property, where it intended to build the retirement home. But those plans never materialized. Instead, the foundation gave the old Buccaneer Hotel on Seawall Boulevard to the Texas Methodist Conference, along with an endowment for renovations. The new facility, then known as The Moody House, was dedicated on Feb. 17, 1962. Bishop Paul E. Martin blessed the building for "happiness, hopefulness, and health that it may ever be a place of peace and joy."

Eventually known as the Edgewater Retirement Community, the building housed Galveston's elderly until 1998. As the building aged, the Methodist Conference struggled to raise the money for restoration. Eventually, they decided to have it demolished, after building a new facility at Seawall Boulevard and 23rd Street. A demolition crew imploded the Buccaneer, to the chagrin of one of the island's most famous restoration advocates—George Mitchell—on Jan. 1, 1999.

CHAPTER SEVEN

Not a natural mother's act

1955

Morris Johnson didn't think twice when Ann Williams drove her light tan car up to his garage in Algoa on Feb. 22, 1955, and asked him to bury four packages of spoiled venison. The mechanic met the young mother and her husband, Hoyt, when he worked on their car the previous fall. When Williams learned Johnson's wife was sick, she stayed with the woman for three days, tenderly nursing her back to health.

So, Johnson was only too happy to help Williams dispose of the ruined meat. She backed her car into the field behind his shop, stopped at a hollow depression, and opened the trunk. One of the packages had started to leak, and Williams quickly threw her jacket over it, scooping it up and placing it in the hole herself. Johnson and his son, Clayton, carried the other packages. Williams asked them to leave her coat covering the package she had carried, saying it was old and she no longer needed it. Once the men had covered the parcels with a layer of dirt, Johnson and his wife asked Williams to stay for dinner. It wasn't until the family sat down to eat that they thought to ask about Williams' two young sons—9-year-old Calvin and 8-year-old Conrad. They were at home in Pasadena, she said, and no trouble at all because they could fix their own supper.

The Johnsons accepted her explanation, although they later admitted it was a little strange. During dinner, Williams talked about the children and how they loved watching television. She gave no indication anything was wrong. But after she left, one of Johnson's mechanics, Gene Wetmore, came in the house with a copy of the evening newspaper. It contained a story about a missing five-and-dime store clerk and her two young children. They looked at each other with wide eyes when they read her name—Ann Williams.

"I told him right off, 'I bet you buried that woman's kids,'" Wetmore told Galveston Daily News reporter George Belk the next day. "We went out to look and then called the police."

Sheriff's deputies arrested Williams a few hours later. After five hours of questioning, she confessed to murdering the boys. They had suffered unbearable teasing from their classmates because their father was serving a three-year term in an Atlanta prison for transporting a stolen car across state lines, Williams claimed. She said she planned to kill the boys to put them out of their misery, then take her own life. She measured out three doses of sleeping pills she had purchased in Mexico, never expecting to wake up. When she did, she discovered the boys were still breathing. So, she took a handkerchief, wrapped it around their slender necks and twisted it with a nail, tourniquet-style, until the rise and fall of their little chests stopped.

Then she had a problem: how to dispose of the bodies? She told investigators she took the bodies to an apartment she had rented in Houston. She filled the bathtub with water, lime, and lye and let the bodies sit for three days. When they didn't disintegrate, she claimed she used a safety razor blade to cut them into pieces, wrapping them in plastic, and storing them in her "electric ice box." Three days after that, she drove them to Algoa.

"I had to hide them," she explained in a jailhouse interview. "I didn't want people to think I was a bad mother."

Investigators, led by Galveston County Deputy Sheriff Curt Monceaux, to whom Williams confessed, immediately began searching for a possible male accomplice. She denied having help to kill the boys, but the county pathologist determined they died from repeated blows to the head. He found no evidence of sleeping pills in their stomachs. Williams denied ever striking her children.

"I believe Mrs. Williams is protecting someone," Monceaux said.

Investigators didn't name the possible accomplice, but Williams admitted to having a boyfriend and planning to leave her husband. She insisted her lover was not involved in the murders.

"If he were mixed up in this, I wouldn't love him," she said. "I couldn't love anybody that would get mixed up in something like this."

Police interviewed two men who knew Williams, but they released both without charges. One, a 27-year-old truck driver, said he met Williams at a Christmas dance and had visited her home several times. She told him she was going to send the boys to a private school in Illinois and when she returned from dropping them off, he said she planned to use a different name. Investigators believed she hatched the murder plan after meeting the man, hoping to start a new life free from her children.

Monceaux, an experienced lawman and former intelligence officer during World War II, described the Williams murders as "the most grotesque case in my career as a law officer."

During her jailhouse interview with The Daily News, Williams said she could justify the murders at the time but not any longer.

"I've prayed for forgiveness," she sobbed. "But I doubt if He can forgive me. Will I ever forget this? Why, oh why, did I do it? Why did I turn on my children?"

The Harris County psychiatrist who interviewed Williams shortly after her arrest said her statements proved her sanity: "She realizes her guilt and expects to be punished."

"I don't know why I killed them. I loved them," Williams said, growing hysterical as she recounted to the reporter what happened. "Take me to the electric chair! I don't mind any more."

~ ~ ~ ~ ~

Famous Houston attorney Percy Foreman held a news conference at the Galveston State Psychiatric Hospital on March 25, 1955, to announce he had agreed to defend Ann Williams in her upcoming murder trials.

"I don't think she's sound of mind now, and I don't think she was sane then," he told reporters. "It's not a natural mother's act."

A Galveston County grand jury indicted Williams on two counts of murder almost exactly one month after she buried the dismembered bodies of her two young sons behind the Algoa auto shop. Although Williams initially confessed to the murders, she recanted just a few days after the indictments.

Williams, the 28-year-old five-and-dime store clerk alternately described in news accounts as "attractive" and "comely," initially said she strangled the boys to stop the suffering they endured from their classmates' teasing. She also said she didn't want to see them grow up in poverty, as she had. But after spending a few weeks in jail and at the Galveston State Psychiatric Hospital, she began to blame the murders on a "junkie" drug dealer who sent her away from her Pasadena trailer and killed the boys in her absence.

During his news conference, Foreman stood next to Williams' mother, sister, and a family friend to announce his defense strategy: insanity. But Galveston County Attorney Marsene Johnson Jr. told The Galveston Daily News the doctors evaluating Williams had yet to establish a definite diagnosis. Beyond that, Johnson wasn't talking.

"We don't try our cases in the newspapers," he said. "We try them in court. Everything she stated in her confession can be backed up by numbers of witnesses."

Some of those witnesses testified during Williams' habeas corpus hearing, which began on April 5. Williams pleaded not guilty. Although the contents of her confession had been widely reported, Foreman didn't have a copy. He repeatedly tried to have it admitted into evidence, claiming it was the sole basis for the state's case against his client and that its contents would be repudiated by witnesses. But he lost his bid to get Johnson to show his "ace card." Judge W.E. Stone ruled the state did not have to produce the evidence until trial, tentatively scheduled for the end of May. Foreman also lost his attempt to get Williams freed on bail.

But the hearing wasn't a total loss for the defense. Foreman, described by The Daily News as "a spectacular Houston courtroom performer," put on a show to help prove his client couldn't be held accountable for whatever she had done. Before the hearing began, he escorted her through the courtroom door, where her mother embraced her before bursting into tears. As the lawyers argued over her fate, Williams sat at a table and rested her head on her arms, apparently oblivious to everything going on around her. Several times, Stone asked Foreman whether she was asleep. Each time, Foreman rose from his chair and bent over her, straightening up after a few moments to announce that she was awake. Later in the morning, she lay back in her chair and appeared to have dozed off—until she fainted, slumping into the lap of Foreman's assistant. When Stone called a recess, Foreman scooped up his client and carried her into the judge's office to be revived. As he questioned witnesses, Foreman repeatedly referred to Williams as "this little lady" or "this little girl."

Although Williams' trial was scheduled to begin about six weeks after the habeas corpus hearing, 1955 proved to be a particularly busy year for murder trials. Johnson had to juggle the prosecution of two other sensational killers—Ellis Lauhon (see Chapter 1) and Robert Wallace (see Chapter 6). Both the prosecution and the defense asked for delays, postponing the trial for six more months.

Williams finally went to trial on Nov. 7. As he had before, Foreman escorted her into the courtroom, where her grey-haired mother greeted her with tears and an embrace. A pool of 300 prospective jurors had been called to the courthouse, about one-third of them women. It was the first time in Galveston County history that women had been called to serve as jurors in a murder trial. Quite a few of the women asked to be excused because they had young children. One even had her young son in the courtroom with her. If the boy's presence bothered Williams, she showed no sign.

The first prospective juror interviewed was a widow from La Marque, who admitted she had an opinion on the case. She was promptly dismissed. As the second juror was being questioned, Johnson and Foreman stood together to make a surprise announcement—Williams had agreed to a plea deal. Facing the possibility of a death sentence, the confessed killer decided to plead guilty in exchange for life in prison. The announcement sent a ripple of shock through the packed courtroom. Even the judge admitted it was a most unusual circumstance.

Despite the plea, jury selection continued, with the prospective jurors now asked whether they would approve the deal. It didn't take long to find 12 people—seven men and five women—who agreed. They listened to a few witnesses relate the undisputed facts of the case and quickly returned their verdict. The foreman, retired school teacher Alice Block, pronounced Williams guilty of the first murder. Jury selection then began for the second trial, which included almost exactly the same testimony. This time, the jurors took much longer to reach a decision. About half way through an hour and a half of deliberations, they sent a message to the judge with a question about sentencing: Would William serve her life terms concurrently? He told them they couldn't consider the facts or disposition of any other case in reaching their conclusion. After they returned their verdict, the jurors learned Williams would serve her sentences concurrently and could be eligible for parole in as little as 15 years.

During his re-election bid the following spring, Johnson faced accusations of bungling the Williams case. But his chances of seeing her sent to the electric chair were slim. Since 1939, Galveston County juries had imposed the death penalty only three times, none for a woman, according to The Daily News. And at that time, no woman had ever been executed in Texas. The only woman on death row in the state up to that point had her sentence commuted to life in prison.

When asked why he had agreed to the deal, Johnson cited "the facts and circumstances of the case" but didn't elaborate. Foreman declined to comment. During his trial arguments, he told jurors a psychiatrist in Beaumont had given Williams sodium pentathol, or "truth serum," and asked her about the murders. Under the influence of the drug, when the doctor insisted she couldn't lie, Williams said she didn't kill the boys. But the doctor, according to Foreman, believed Williams was present when they were killed and dismembered, making her culpable and deserving of punishment. Unfortunately, for Foreman and Williams, none of that evidence was admissible in court.

Galveston County officials transferred Williams to the Goree State Prison on Nov. 17.

CHAPTER EIGHT

The body in the Fort San Jacinto bunker

1960

Several hours after the hot sun melted into the horizon on Aug. 21, 1960, three 13-year-old boys ran along a narrow strip of sand on Galveston's far East End. They were supposed to be fishing, but a torrential summer downpour drove them toward a bunker at old Fort San Jacinto. The gaping black entrance to the crumbling fortress, built in the early 1900s, probably seemed like it offered endless opportunities for adventure. But the three Boy Scouts from Houston had no idea their night's excitement would make them witnesses in a murder investigation.

As they felt their way into the abandoned bunker, the boys stumbled across the body of a dead woman. Her hands were folded across her chest, and a cross made out of two bamboo sticks rested on her stomach. In the sand nearby someone had scratched a message: "I dide (sic) not want to kill her. Roy told. Tell mama I love her very much."

The boys fled back to the beach where the father of one of them drove to the police station.

The woman turned out to be Mildred "Sandy" Ferro, a 32-year-old waitress at the Idle Hour Club, 1903 Tremont. Seven hours before the boys found her body, Sandy's estranged husband stormed into the club waving a gun.

"Don't give me any trouble, or you'll all go," he told the half dozen patrons. They watched helplessly as John Ferro grabbed his wife around the waist and dragged her out the front door. She screamed and struggled as her husband and another man forced her into a waiting car that sped away, witnesses told police.

One bystander took down the car's license plate number, which eventually led police to the Texas City home of 20-year-old Orlen Block. Detectives found a bullet fragment in the back seat and blood-soaked floor mats. After questioning Block, Texas City police also arrested Domingo Williams, 25.

In Galveston, police knocked on the door of Ferro's 12th Street apartment. When he didn't answer, they looked in the window. Ferro was lying in bed, blood seeping from a hole in his temple. They pried open the front door with a tire iron and ordered him to roll over and drop the gun. He did, immediately, but he didn't seem to realize it.

"Go ahead, take my gun," he said, holding out an empty, bloody hand for several seconds after the gun fell to the floor. "Take my gun!"

At John Sealy Hospital, doctors discovered the .32-caliber bullet with which Ferro tried to kill himself passed through his head with minimal harm. The only damage appeared to be to the optical nerve, which it severed, leaving Ferro completely blind. Next to the bed in the apartment, investigators found a note:

"Sandy cause this Mama. Mama everything I got go to you. Sandy got me in the hold so bad that this is the only way out. So try to get Pete out to see me and God bless you for me, Mama. Sorry Mama."

The couple's trouble began not long after they married. In August 1939, Sandy filed charges against her husband for beating and threatening her. The justice of the peace who heard the case later testified the new bride appeared desperately afraid of her husband. Sandy soon filed for divorce, but it wasn't final by the time she died.

Despite her attempts to get away from him, Ferro continued to act as though Sandy belonged to him. Roy Brock, who operated the Idle Hour Club, later testified Ferro told him just a few weeks before the murder he had two men from Houston who were going to help him "straighten her out." Brock said Ferro told him he was no longer going to sea and couldn't afford to live on what Sandy made at the club. He said he planned to take her north and put her in a house of prostitution.

In his confession to police, Orlen Block said after he and Ferro snatched Sandy from the club on Aug. 21, Ferro began pistol-whipping her in the back seat of the car. About four blocks from the club, Block and Williams heard a gunshot.

"I asked Johnny, 'Did you shoot her?'" Williams later recalled. "And he said, 'No, I just hit her in the head and the gun went off. She's just knocked out.'"

With Sandy slumped over in the back seat, Ferro told Williams to drive to Fort San Jacinto. When they arrived, he dragged her out of the car, telling Block to pick up her feet. Block insisted Sandy was still alive, stumbling into the bunker with her arm around Ferro's neck. But Ferro came back out of the bunker alone and handed Block and Williams his wife's wedding ring, telling them to hock it for as much as possible and meet him later. The two men drove away and said they had no idea what happened to Sandy after that.

According to the autopsy, Sandy died of a gunshot wound to the head. Based on the lack of blood in the bunker, police believed she either died in the car or shorty after Ferro dumped her in the fort.

The three men were scheduled for trial at the end of January 1961. As jury selection got underway, Ferro pleaded guilty to murder and agreed to accept a life sentence. Block and Williams took their chances with a jury, getting 25 years each. They left for Huntsville together but Ferro didn't stay there long. According to a funeral announcement in The Galveston Daily News, he died in February 1964, coming home to be buried on the island.

CHAPTER NINE

Buried alive on the Bolivar Peninsula

1980

Suzanne Clydene Knuth trudged home alone in the dark on April 4, 1980, after her car died in a Beaumont shopping center parking lot. The 23-year-old Lamar University student didn't have far to walk, and the short distance probably didn't seem like a big deal.

But as she approached an auto body shop, a newer-model Oldsmobile Cutlass pulled up to the curb next to her and a lanky man got out.

Dee Ann Barthell, a 17-year-old high school student driving to a local disco, watched the ensuing scuffle unfold.

"He had her by the back of the neck and by the hair," Barthell later testified in a Galveston County courtroom.

Jerry Atkins, who worked at the auto body shop, heard the commotion and came outside to see what was going on.

"This guy was beatin' up on her and she was screamin' for help. I thought the guy might have a gun or it was a family argument and that's not something I meddle in," said Atkins, the last person besides her killer to see Knuth alive.

The attacker eventually forced Knuth into his car and sped away.

~ ~ ~ ~ ~

Around midnight, 32-year-old Chester Lee Wicker, a former Marine and out-of-work handyman, got his mom's Oldsmobile stuck in the sand near Crystal Beach. His uncle, Bob Wicker, lived nearby and helped pull the car free. He noticed blood on the floor mats and smeared on his nephew's shirt. Wicker said he'd cut his arm. His uncle didn't ask any more questions.

Two days later, on Easter Sunday, Wicker posed for a family photograph with his wife and young daughter. Then he took his wife's car and drove west, eventually arriving April 11 in El Centro, Calif., where he dropped in on another uncle. Five days later, he called his cousin from a town in northern Washington state, near the Canadian border. He told her he'd left his wife's car in Los Angeles and hitchhiked north. But he wanted to come home. She wired him money for a bus ticket back to El Centro, where he arrived on April 20.

While Wicker wandered across the country, Barthell agreed to be hypnotized in hopes it would help her remember details about Knuth's attacker. Initially, the teen identified a photograph of Knuth's husband, Calvin. But after her hypnosis, she picked Wicker out of a photo line-up.

Unaware Beaumont police were closing in, Wicker decided it was time to come home. Less than 24 hours after arriving in El Centro, he boarded another bus headed for Texas. Before he left, he told his cousin he'd fled Beaumont because "he was in trouble and might have to go to prison." After the bus pulled out of the station, Wicker's cousin called the police.

Officers from Beaumont were waiting with handcuffs when Wicker stepped off the bus in Houston around midnight April 21. The next day, Wicker confessed to kidnapping Knuth and burying her body about 1.5 miles east of the Crystal Beach city limits, on property owned by Sun Oil.

"I got a shell and used it and my hands to dig a hole as long as she was," Wicker said in his confession.

Investigators found Knuth's body April 22 in a shallow grave. She was wearing only socks, a ripped blouse and a bra pulled up over her breasts. Wicker claimed Knuth tried to escape from the car as they drove down the Bolivar Peninsula, hitting her head when she jumped or fell out the door. He said he checked for a heartbeat and a pulse before digging her grave.

But the medical examiner found sand "throughout" Knuth's lungs, evidence she was still alive when Wicker buried her. A Galveston grand jury indicted him on capital murder charges.

~ ~ ~ ~ ~

In October, District Judge Larry Gist, who came from Beaumont to preside over the trial in Galveston, ruled Wicker had been arrested illegally because the police at that time didn't have probable cause to detain him. But the judge ruled Wicker's confession admissible and ordered his court-appointed attorneys to prepare their defense. Two months later, Wicker appeared before a seven-woman, five-man Galveston County jury.

His lawyers challenged the hypnosis testimony and petitioned for a mistrial after court employees overheard jurors talking about the case —against the judge's orders—during lunch at a local Mexican restaurant. But Wicker's confessions left little for them to work with. He never took the stand in his own defense.

After listening to six days of testimony, jurors deliberated for four hours and 45 minutes before finding Wicker guilty of capital murder.

During the sentencing phase, prosecutors revealed Wicker had pleaded guilty to rape charges in 1971 and 1973 and to assault in 1977. One of the rapes, which also took place at Crystal Beach, bore striking similarities to Knuth's murder. The victim, a woman from Alabama who was vacationing on Bolivar at the time of the attack, recounted how Wicker tied her hands behind her back, pushed her to the ground and pulled her shirt up. He didn't succeed in raping her—but he tried.

Prosecutors asked for the death penalty after reading from a list of Wicker's victims: "Remember Suzanne Cyldene Knuth in your deliberations and sentence Chester Lee Wicker to death so when you look in the mirror tomorrow morning you will know that no names will be added to this list."

The jury took just two hours to agree to the death sentence, deciding Wicker deliberately killed Knuth and had a high likelihood of committing violent crimes in the future. One of Wicker's defense attorneys called the verdict "not unexpected."

Gist set Wicker's execution date for Aug. 11, 1984. The Texas Court of Criminal Appeals upheld the sentence in February, but the Supreme Court granted a stay on July 23. On Oct. 9, the high court cleared the way for the execution to proceed in February, 1985. Wicker continued to appeal his case, winning another temporary stay a week before his second execution date. The federal court in Galveston agreed to hear arguments from the ACLU claiming the testimony based on Barthell's hypnosis session should never have been presented at trial. Prosecutors argued the teen's eyewitness account made little difference in the outcome after Wicker confessed and led police to the body.

While admitting the unreliability of hypnosis, U.S. District Court Judge Hugh Gibson upheld Wicker's sentence and set a new date with death.

Wicker died Aug. 26, 1986, by lethal injection. According to a short Associated Press report, he threw "a tantrum" in his cell earlier in the day but went calmly to the death chamber. He had just one witness present, a "friend and spiritual adviser" to whom he mouthed "I love you" as the lethal drugs began coursing through his veins.

CHAPTER TEN

Seawall attacker guts victim 'like a fish'

1970

After spending a fun night out, best friends Judy Mills, 21, and Susan Perry, 20, walked home together down the seawall at about 1 a.m. on Oct. 31, 1970. When they reached 22nd Street, they warily watched a man cross the street and start walking in the same direction, about 10 paces in front of them.

They slowed. He slowed.

Nervous, the girls kept walking until they had almost caught up with the man. When he was only about five feet in front of them, he whirled around. Before they could react, he grabbed both girls around their waists and the tangled trio tumbled over the seawall. Each girl screamed the other's name as they fell. Perry managed to grab the edge with one hand, slowing her descent and wresting herself free from her attacker. After she dropped onto the granite boulders below, she spotted her friend lying motionless nearby. The man crouched over her.

Looking up, he calmly told her what he had planned: He would rape her first and then come back for her friend.

Perry ran toward 25th Street, the attacker's feet pounding out a rapid staccato on the sand behind her. When he stumbled, she widened the gap between them. She knew she'd escaped when she reached the base of the stairs leading to the sidewalk. She scrambled up and flagged down the first car she saw.

The driver, AJ Rodriguez, knew both girls and immediately pulled over to help. While his friend took Perry across the street to the Golden Greek to call police, Rodriguez ran down to the beach to look for Mills. He found her, splayed half naked on the rocks where she had fallen, gasping for air. Her attacker had slashed her throat and cut a deep gash from her stomach to her chest. Rodriguez later testified she was cut "just like you would gut a fish."

Medics rushed Mills to John Sealy Hospital where doctors pronounced her dead. Police took Perry to the station to help an artist make a sketch of the attacker. A few hours later, a detective patrolling on 21st Street near the courthouse spotted a station waggon that matched the description of a car mentioned in several recent complaints about a man exposing himself on the UTMB campus.

After his arrest, Haskell Leroy Willoughby, a 37-year-old welder working for Kelso Marine, refused to talk. Investigators found plenty to incriminate him: a pair of bloodstained shoes in his car and a bag of bloody clothes in an alley nearby. But Perry couldn't pick him out of a lineup seven hours after the attack. Police meanwhile learned Willoughby was wanted in Austin for exposing himself to a minor. About 43 hours after the attack, Perry did pick Willoughby out of a second lineup.

District Attorney Jules Damiani quickly charged him with murder and announced plans to seek the death penalty.

The trial began April 27, 1971. Defense attorneys immediately tried to discredit Perry's testimony, noting her initial inability to ID the attacker. They also noted Willoughby was the only man who appeared in both lineups Perry reviewed, suggesting she might have recognized him from the first attempt, not from the attack. Three other people driving down Seawall Boulevard at the time of the attack, one who saw the trio tumble over the edge and a couple who watched the attacker cross the street shortly afterward, also failed to positively identify Willoughby.

Still, police had the bloody clothes, which should have been a prosecutorial slam dunk. But as the trial's second day began, investigators dropped a bombshell: the forensic team in Austin couldn't type the blood, leaving prosecutors with no way to tie the items to Willoughby or the murder. They also had to admit Willoughby had a boil on his scrotum, which defense attorneys argued could have left the bloodstains on his clothes and the sheets in his hotel room.

In another setback for the prosecution, three witnesses called to testify about Willoughby's actions shortly before and after the murder said they didn't think him capable of such a violent act. Ron Nicholson, one of Willoughby's coworkers from Kelso Marine, testified the two had gone to a club together the night of the murder, ending the evening with a stop at Betty's Grill, at 39th and Ave. S. Shortly after they sat down at a table, Willoughby excused himself, saying he'd be right back. Mills and Perry were attacked about 30 minutes later. Nicholson said Willoughby appeared perfectly normal, although he never returned to the restaurant.

Pat Evans, the desk clerk at the motel where Willoughby lived, described him as a quiet man who didn't cause trouble. Hilda Irene Jacobson, a waitress at another restaurant Willoughby frequented, described him as a "perfect gentleman." She even admitted to going on two dates with him, during which he didn't do anything wrong. When she saw him the morning after the murder, he seemed fine, except that he had a limp. He explained it by saying he had gotten drunk and wrecked his motorcycle the previous evening. Police said he injured his leg in the fall over the seawall.

Defense attorneys tried to make the most of those positive accounts of Willoughby. They were the only ones. Six women took the stand and identified Willoughby as the man who exposed himself to them while they walked on or near UTMB. One woman said he grabbed her from behind when she was walking down Ave. I between 7th and 8th streets. She hit him twice in the face with her purse and he fled. Two coworkers from Kelso Marine testified Willoughby had a "bad temper" and one said he had seen Willoughby in a fight.

Despite the prosecution's struggle to make a direct connection between Willoughby and the murder, the defense team dropped claims of their client's innocence when it came time to make their case. They mounted an insanity defense instead, telling jurors Willoughby couldn't be held accountable for his actions that night. Defense attorney Robert Coltzer claimed Willoughby had struggled since childhood with a mental illness that "compels him to a state of frustration, a state of excitement, a state in which he cannot control himself." Coltzer claimed Willoughby could not tell the difference between right and wrong when he attacked women.

Willoughby had at one time been confined to the Austin State Mental Hospital in 1958 for treatment. A psychiatrist who treated him then testified Willoughby had a very severe case of antisocial behavior that filled him with "inner tension and hostilities." Willoughby's mother, Rena Milburn, testified he hadn't caused any trouble except that sometimes he complained of headaches and would leave the house. Then police would come and say he'd been accused of exposing himself.

To counter the insanity defense, prosecutors produced three psychiatrists who testified Willoughby was mentally ill but not legally insane because he could tell the difference between right and wrong. One described his sociopathic disorder as a behavior problem, not a mental illness.

The jury deliberated for two hours and 10 minutes before finding Willoughby guilty. But jurors seemed to struggle with his punishment. Defense attorney Hulen Selman argued hard against the death penalty. He insisted it wasn't a deterrent to crime but would only serve as a "vendetta," which he urged the jury not to pursue "in the defense of civilization."

"This man will not be put asleep, he will be sizzled and fried," an impassioned Selman told the jury.

Willoughby sat through the trial without ever showing any emotion, even when his own lawyers called him a "miserable, sick little man" and pleaded for his life.

District Attorney Damiani told jurors putting Willoughby to death was the only way to ensure he didn't hurt anyone else: "I can tell you that this man must be removed permanently from society for the protection of society. He's not going to conform to society, in fact he'll go out and do it again."

The jury deliberated for another seven hours and 45 minutes before returning a death sentence.

Willoughby spent three years on death row before the U.S. Supreme Court declared the death penalty unconstitutional, commuting his sentence to life in prison. In 1983, the Texas Parole Board considered releasing Willoughby, but Mills' family and friends successfully lobbied the board to keep him behind bars. He died while still in prison, in 2016.

CHAPTER ELEVEN

Shootout shatters Texas City love triangle

1966

Love can drive a man to distraction. But can it make him a murderer?

Richard Villareal's attorneys insisted it could. He was a man whose life was wrapped up in a woman, entangled in a web he could not escape. His lawyers painted the picture of a pitiable victim pushed to the breaking point by a heartless woman. They didn't deny his deadly actions but argued he shouldn't be held responsible.

On May 28, 1966, Villareal burst through the backdoor into the kitchen of the home at 4015 18th Avenue in Texas City. Without saying a word, he started shooting, hitting Wiley Rogers Barganier four times. Barganier's wife of two weeks, Charlene, ran into the living room to call police. Villareal chased her down, catching up with her before she could dial the number. He ripped the receiver from her hand, threw her on the couch, and pointed the gun at her face.

Then he pulled the trigger.

The bullet entered near her chin and exited through her neck. Bleeding profusely, Charlene struggled with her attacker, eventually breaking away and running into the bedroom—where she found her own gun. Villareal's defense attorney later asked where she planned to shoot his client.

"I was just shooting," she recalled. "I didn't care where I shot."

Only one of Charlene's .22-caliber bullets hit its mark, striking Villareal in the right shoulder. She ran out the door, through the yard to a neighbor's house, where she called for help.

Galveston County District Attorney Jules Damiani charged Villareal, a 46-year-old marine engineer, with murder with malice aforethought. He pleaded not guilty, and when he stood before a jury 16 months later, his defense team put Charlene on trial.

The two first met in 1964, when they were both married to other people. But they began seeing each other whenever they could. Under some very direct questioning by defense attorney Clyde Woody, Charlene admitted she and Villareal began sleeping together in September 1964. They first met at motels in Kemah, Beaumont, New Orleans, and Texas City. Later, Charlene became such a constant presence at Villareal's apartment that the manager assumed they were married. Villareal's wife died in October 1964, and Charlene finally divorced her husband in April 1965.

A few months later, she began seeing Barganier, along with other men.

Charlene admitted she had been engaged to Villareal but broke it off four times. She insisted Villareal knew how she felt, recalling a conversation they had in early 1966.

"He asked me if I was going to marry him this year and I said no," she testified. "He asked if I was gonna marry him next year and I said no. He asked if I was ever gonna marry him. I said no."

When Barganier asked her to marry him in December 1965, she told him about Villareal. She claimed both men knew where they stood. Woody offered a different perspective.

"You played one man against the other," he told her in a packed Galveston County courtroom.

The Galveston Daily News described Woody's questioning as a "scathing attack." He asserted Villareal was trying to "make an honest woman" of Charlene, and she "drove him right out of his mind." Woody worked hard to convince jurors a common-law marriage existed between the couple, which would have forced them to disregard all of Charlene's testimony.

Although Charlene insisted they were not married, Villareal testified he considered her his wife, in practice if not by law. He gave her money for household expenses, and they lived together like man and wife. He suspected nothing when she took him to Baytown for his last trip to sea on May 8, 1966, promising she would pick him up when he got back to port. But when he called from Florida to tell her the ship was headed home, she bluntly announced an end to their domestic bliss. She'd married Barganier shortly after Villareal's vessel sailed out of the Houston Ship Channel. She told him to come collect his things from her house as soon as he disembarked.

Crushed, Villareal had a friend pick up him up at the port and take him to Charlene's house. Then he retreated to his apartment and started drinking. He later recalled he only emerged when his bottle ran dry. He even hung a do-not-disturb sign on his door. He testified he had no memory of the night he walked into Charlene's house and began shooting. He vaguely remembered buying the gun earlier that day but claimed he didn't intend to kill anyone.

During closing arguments, Woody's assistant, Mariam Rosen, told jurors Villareal could not have been of sound mind at the time of the murder. She blamed Charlene for what happened that night.

"What kind of woman plays with the emotions of those who love her?" Rosen asked. "He wasn't himself. Poor, tormented soul, his heart burning for the woman he loved."

Damiani called Villareal's amnesia claims "hogwash." He said if that argument held, anyone could get drunk, shoot someone, and go free. Jurors evidently agreed. After five hours deliberation, they declared Villareal guilty. After another seven hours, they sentenced him to 15 years in prison.

During his closing arguments, Damiani said the power of love has it limits: "Love is precious, the defense says; but I submit that life is precious, too."

CHAPTER TWELVE

Honest, officer, I'm trying to go straight!

1927

On Nov. 1, 1927, teller Chester Griffin was sitting at the counter of First National Bank in Texas City when two men walked in waving guns. One of the men ordered Griffin and bookkeeper Elizabeth Lege to stand against the back wall while the other ran into the vault and started sweeping stacks of bills into a bag. The robbers locked Griffin and Lege in the vault before speeding away in a Buick sedan.

They made off with about $6,000—the equivalent of almost $83,000 today.

Police brought Griffin in to look through photographs of criminals, and he picked one well-known robber out of the lineup. W.S. "Shiloh" Scrivnor, then 32 years old, had already had an illustrious career that included several spectacular heists and a stint in prison. Texas City Police Chief A.E. Addison assured Griffin that Scrivnor was a very bad man.

Two weeks after the Texas City robbery, police knocked on the door of Scrivnor's Houston home just before midnight. He was in his pajamas, just about to turn in for the night. The officers brought him to Galveston, where Griffin identified him in person. The other well-known robber identified in the photo lineup, Johnny Martin, could not be located.

Scrivnor—who swore he was trying to go straight—proclaimed his innocence. And so began one of the longest legal battles in Galveston County history.

Newspaper reports detailing Scrivnor's exploits described him as debonair, and his early life gave no indication of his future criminal enterprise. He grew up "in the shadow of the Capitol dome" in Austin, according to his Galveston attorney, L.M. Kenyon. He even spent some time as a page in the Texas House of Representatives. He briefly considered going into the ministry but evidently found robbing banks more appealing than preaching.

While still in his teens, Scrivnor was convicted in Dallas for the Sanger Bros. payroll robbery. The jury gave him a 50-year sentence. But he escaped after two years and managed to evade being recaptured until he joined the gang that robbed the Jackson Street post office in 1917. Dallas police caught him with $1 million in securities, still in their mail sacks, when the car he was in crashed into a telephone pole. The driver died on impact, and Scrivnor woke up in the hospital, surrounded by police officers. During the 36 months he spent in a Dallas jail, Scrivnor was convicted of robbing First State Bank in Oak Cliff. But he was pardoned in exchange for his testimony in the post office case.

After gaining his freedom, Scrivnor moved to Houston and sold newspaper advertising—until Texas City police arrested him.

Scrivnor stood trial in Galveston a month after the Texas City robbery. Jurors convicted and sentenced him to 99 years in prison. But Scrivnor's attorneys demanded a new trial after they learned one of the jurors claimed he was coerced into voting to convict. His attorneys also claimed the indictment unfairly referenced the previous conviction for which Scrivnor was pardoned. Judge C.G. Dibrell denied the motion for a new trial, but five months later the Court of Criminal Appeals in Austin overturned the verdict. Galveston prosecutors fought the decision, and it would take another 15 months for the appeals court to uphold its decision.

While Scrivnor fought for a new trial, police captured Martin in Texarkana, where he had fled to escape police in Birmingham after robbing a hotel there. He agreed to go back to Galveston but said he would fight extradition to Alabama. A Galveston jury convicted Martin for the Texas City robbery and gave him a 25-year sentence in July 1929.

Scrivnor went back to court on Nov. 15, 1929, for a bond hearing. The Galveston Tribune reporter covering the trial described him as "dressed in a natty and freshly pressed sand-colored suit, with a necktie embellished with a glittering diamond stickpin." Five Dallas residents had agreed to put up a $10,000 bond to get Scrivnor out of jail during the trial. The sheriff refused to accept it until Dibrell ruled he couldn't deny Scrivnor his freedom.

The second trial didn't begin until July 1, 1930. The defense team presented an impressive parade of witnesses who claimed to have seen or talked to Scrivnor in Houston on the day of the robbery. A Houston police detective working as a mounted traffic officer even testified to seeing Scrivnor outside a store where he purchased some insecticide to kill the sand fleas plaguing his back yard. Scrivnor's wife, who was about three months pregnant, staunchly defended her husband and said the police had constantly hounded him, even though he was trying to live honestly.

The state's star witness was an ex-convict who'd known Scrivnor in prison. M.M. McDaniel claimed Scrivnor and Martin visited him in Galveston several days before the robbery and asked about Texas City police patrols and escape routes. Scrivnor denied having anything to do with McDaniel, whom he described as a "dope" addict.

"Since I got out of trouble, I've been trying to live honest," Scrivnor said on the stand. "It wouldn't be right for my wife if I were associated with a drug addict. I wouldn't be in the habit of seeking out ex-convicts because I'm trying to make an honest living."

Jurors deliberated for 32 hours before declaring themselves hopelessly deadlocked. Eight men voted to acquit Scrivnor and four voted to convict—on every ballot the group took from the beginning of its deliberations.

After another year of freedom, Scrivnor returned to Galveston in May 1931 for a third trial. This time, the jury convicted him and gave him a 10-year sentence. His attorneys again appealed to the Court of Criminal Appeals, alleging gross jury misconduct. While awaiting the outcome of his appeal, Scrivnor was arrested in Des Moines, Iowa, after his partner died in a gun battle with police. Houston prosecutors returned him to Texas to stand trial for the murder of C.A. "Keggy" Jones and his wife, Jane, who were shot in their Montrose apartment in retaliation for killing one of Scrivnor's associates.

While he was jailed in Houston, prosecutors in Tennessee indicted Scrivnor for robbing a Memphis bank. He also faced a murder charge for killing a well-known cattleman in a Hot Springs, Ark., hotel—until prosecutors there realized he was behind bars at the time of the shooting. A Houston jury acquitted Scrivnor of killing Jane Jones, and prosecutors gave up on trying him for the husband's murder. Instead, they sent him back to Galveston to begin serving his 10-year bank robbery sentence.

Galveston sheriff's deputies escorted Scrivnor to Huntsville in June 1932. Gov. Miriam "Ma" Ferguson, a well-known friend to prisoners, granted Scrivnor a short furlough in 1934, extending it when Dallas investigators picked him up to talk about another post office robbery. He spent three more years in prison, getting out on May 7, 1937, after serving just shy of half his sentence. When prison officials set him free, Scrivnor had a statement prepared for the press.

"I am anxious to go straight," he said. "I know the feathers of a jail bird are poor apparel in which to seek recognition of one's real worth. This attitude of men is the greatest barrier to the men discharged from prison. What will I do? I don't know yet. I simply want to make good. I want to live my past down. I hope you will let me."

Scrivnor managed to stay out of trouble until February 1941, when police arrested him on weapons charges. Houston detectives spotted

Scrivnor and Vernon Hancock, another ex-con, sitting in a parked car. In the truck the officers found two guns, which were illegal for the men to have since they had previous violent crime convictions. The detectives also found a pair of bolt cutters, a heavy sledge hammer, three steel punches, a pair of cutting pliers, two pinch bars, two files, and a 20-foot rope ladder.

CHAPTER THIRTEEN

Suspicions of incest trigger deadly family feud

1930

Twelve-year-old Donald Sedgewick trotted down the steps of his grandfather's house to get a piece of apple pie from a family friend who had stopped by during the early evening of Nov. 6, 1930. Just as he hit the sidewalk, a gray sedan rolled up to the house. He recognized it immediately as his father's, and it sent him running back inside. He grabbed his mother and pushed her into a back bedroom, where he locked her into a wardrobe. When he heard gunshots, he jumped out the room's back window.

A few minutes later, Donald heard his grandfather, 62-year-old William Ruenbuhl, on the phone with police, telling them his son-in-law was back again—apparently planning to follow through on the threats he'd been making for a week. The police chief dispatched three motorcycle officers to the house, at 1114 33rd Street, but before they arrived, Donald heard more gunfire.

This time, the bullets found their mark. Ruenbuhl lay in a pool of blood in the hallway behind his front door, glass shards covering his body. Next to him rested his double-barreled shotgun.

He never had a chance to fire it.

Donald testified against his father, John B. Sedgewick, in his murder trial, which began on March 18, 1931. Sedgewick's older son, 15-year-old Jack, also testified, recalling the day of his grandmother's funeral, when his father threatened to kill his grandfather. Jack said he begged him not to do it.

When Sedgewick took the stand in his own defense, he claimed the trouble with his father-in-law was 10 years in the making. Ruenbuhl never thought his step-daughter, Blanche, was good enough for Sedgewick. He admitted to threatening Ruenbuhl on the day of his mother-in-law's funeral but suggested it was because something improper was going on between his wife and her step-father.

"If I ever catch you with my wife again, I'll knock your damned head off," he recalled telling Ruenbuhl.

Sedgewick, who lived in Houston at the time of the murder, admitted to having a troubled marriage—separating from his wife 13 times. When asked why his wife left him, Sedgewick refused to answer, saying he would rather "burn" than say a word against her. But he admitted to being "a fool and a beggar."

Earlier that year, Sedgewick spent four months in John Sealy Hospital for an undisclosed illness. When prosecutors put his doctor on the stand to testify to his mental state, Sedgewick's attorney, L.M. Kenyon, protested, and the judge dismissed the witness. But dozens of people who knew Sedgewick all testified he was not the same after he got out.

"He didn't talk or act as coherently after his visit to the hospital as he did before," acquaintance A.J. Dow testified.

Even Sedgewick's two sisters, who testified in his defense, said he was nervous and worried—worse than he'd ever been before his illness.

But Sedgewick's defense did not involve his mental health, which is why Kenyon didn't want his doctor to testify. Sedgewick claimed he shot Ruenbuhl in self-defense because he thought he was going to hurt Blanche or the children.

While his wife was staying with her step-father, Ruenbuhl refused to let her talk to her husband, Sedgewick claimed. The night of the shooting, Sedgewick went to his brother-in-law's store at 31st and

Ave. P and asked to use the phone. He called Ruenbuhl's house and Blanche answered the phone. Just as he started to talk to her, Sedgewick said she made a choking noise. He thought Ruenbuhl was trying to kill her, he said.

When he arrived at the house, he saw Ruenbuhl standing at the front door. As he approached, Sedgewick said, Ruenbuhl raised a shotgun to his shoulder. Sedgewick said he fired first to avoid being killed himself.

"I'm not a killer," he testified, breaking down in tears on the stand. "I would rather've died than killed Ruenbuhl. I'm not a killer. I wouldn't kill anybody. I almost turned my car over once to avoid hitting a dog."

Sedgewick's sister testified Ruenbuhl told her he was going to kill her brother, bolstering Sedgewick's claim of self-defense. But according to police testimony, Ruenbuhl was the one who feared for his life. He called to report Sedgewick's threats every day for a week before the shooting. The magistrate had even issued a warrant for Sedgewick's arrest.

During closing arguments, prosecutors reminded jurors that police who arrived at the scene had to push Ruenbuhl's body away from the door to open it. If he was standing that close, how could he have raised the shotgun to his shoulder as Sedgewick claimed?

After two and a half days of testimony, jurors retired to consider Sedgewick's fate. Although overflow crowds filled the courtroom throughout the trial, no spectators were left when the jurors reached their verdict at 12:30 a.m. on March 20. Sedgewick could have faced the death penalty, but prosecutors only asked the jury to give him the punishment they thought he deserved. They sentenced him to 20 years. The next day, his attorney said he would not appeal.

But John Sedgewick did not spend the next two decades behind bars.

In March 1933, almost exactly two years after his conviction, Gov. Miriam "Ma" Ferguson pardoned Sedgewick, giving him his freedom.

Ferguson had an infamously liberal pardon policy. Although ostensibly a way to ease overcrowding in Texas prisons, it also was rumored to be a method for making more than a little money on the side. Pardons reportedly could be had in exchange for cash donations to Ferguson's husband, former Gov. James "Pa" Ferguson. During her two terms in office, Ferguson issued 4,000 pardons.

The Galveston Daily News never gave a reason for Sedgewick's pardon.

CHAPTER FOURTEEN

Discrimination claims and Hollywood defense tactics

1946

Charles Ludwig Ueckert sat slumped in his chair at the back of Happy's Newsstand and domino parlor on the night of July 20, 1945. The 69-year-old watchman dozed, apparently unconcerned about the possibility of a robbery. He never saw the fatal blow coming.

His assailant snuck up behind him and wrapped a length of telephone cord around his neck twice, squeezing until he stopped moving. Then he struck the watchman several times on the back of the head with a pool cue, splitting the stick in half with the force of the blows. Ueckert crumpled to the floor. While blood pooled around the watchman's battered head, the robber rifled through the domino parlor's cash drawers, making off with about $700 ($9,200 today) and a mahogany-handled pistol hidden behind the counter.

Painters coming to work on the building at 21114 Market Street the next morning found Ueckert's body. The porter, a 21-year-old African-American man, said the night watchman was alive and well when he left after cleaning up, at about 2:30 a.m. Police speculated whoever carried out the attack knew the place and its routines, waiting to slip inside when they knew Ueckert would be alone. They predicted they would find the killer among the men who hung around outside the place—known as "sidewalk sweaters." But they had few clues to go on, and investigators scrambled for several days to narrow down their list of suspects. They described the killer as a likely petty criminal who killed Ueckert after the watchman recognized him. The lack of any attempt to hide the murder weapons, found in trash cans behind the domino parlor, confirmed the criminal as an unprofessional novice, according to police.

That part was right, but everything else investigators guessed about the killer turned out to be wrong. Four days after Ueckert's body was found, detectives asked James Preston, the domino hall's porter, if they could search his room. In the tiny apartment in the 2500 block of Ave. C, they found $171 and a .38 caliber pistol identified by Joe Rees, domino hall operator, as the one he used to keep behind the counter. Police also found a blood-spattered pair of pants and sent it to the crime lab in Austin for analysis. They arrested Preston and charged him with murder.

After his arrest, Preston admitted to killing Ueckert and taking the money, which he mostly spent in gambling joints around the island. But when he was arraigned before a grand jury several days later, Preston proclaimed his innocence. His attorney, Thomas H. Dent claimed police beat his client into confessing to the crime when they dragged him down to the police station. The grand jury indicted him anyway.

A few days before Preston's trial was set to begin in March, Dent filed a motion to quash the murder indictment, claiming racial discrimination in the selection of the grand jury. No African-American in the history of Galveston had been selected as grand jury commissioner and only one African-American had been selected to sit on a grand jury in the past 30 years, Dent said. Excluding African-Americans from such service because of race and color "is in direct contravention of the 14th Amendment to the Constitution of the United States," he wrote in his motion. Forcing Preston to be judged by an all-white grand jury denied him equal protection and due process, Dent concluded.

The lawyer also made an unsuccessful bid to have Preston declared insane. According to The Galveston Daily News, the accused murderer was encouraged to speak on his own behalf several times throughout the three-hour sanity hearing, but he refused to open his mouth.

He would continue to sit mute all through his trial.

Opening arguments started on March 5, 1946, after the judge rejected Dent's bid to have the indictment quashed. Thirteen witnesses testified for the prosecution, recounting the discovery of Ueckert's body and eventually finding the money and pistol in Preston's room. One of the detectives recalled Preston coming into the domino hall the morning after the murder and exclaiming over the watchman's body.

"Poor Uncle Charlie," he reportedly said.

After his arrest, Preston gave a detailed confession, according to police, who read it to jurors. Preston said he didn't have anything against Ueckert but killed him so he could rob the place. He needed the money because he gambled a lot and was always in the hole, he allegedly told police. And he got the idea to strangle the watchman with telephone wire from a movie he'd seen. After prosecutors rested their case, Dent called Preston to the stand.

"What is your name? Where do you live? Did you know Charles Ueckert? Where was the last place you worked? Do you know you are a defendant in this case? Are these your trousers?"

Preston refused to answer any of his lawyer's questions. He didn't even give any indication he heard them. Tired of asking questions, Dent took the stand to tell jurors Preston had not spoken in the previous six weeks. But a deputy sheriff in charge of transporting Preston testified the prisoner had answered his questions the previous week.

Prosecutors made an impassioned plea for the death penalty, and jurors retired to deliberate shortly after midnight the day after the trial began. It took them 17 hours to reach a verdict, leading many in the courtroom to predict a hung jury. But in the end, the 12 men agreed to send Preston to the state penitentiary for life. When the foreman read the verdict, Preston sat as expressionless as he had through the entire trial.

Seven days later, he returned to the courthouse for his formal sentencing hearing. Judge Charles G. Dibrell told him he owed a lasting debt to Dent, who saved him from the electric chair. At first, Preston didn't speak, until a sheriff's deputy prompted him, noting he'd just been on the phone at the jail. Dibrell asked him if there was any reason he shouldn't be sentenced.

"No sir," he said. "I accept my sentence."

After Dibrell dispatched with several other hearings, he called Preston back into the courtroom to ask him whether he got the idea to sit silent throughout his trial by reading about Rudolf Hess, the Nazi politician who feigned amnesia during his trial at Nuremberg to avoid a death sentence. Preston said he'd read lots of detective stories, watched a lot of movies and "made a study of it."

"In other words, you just put on an act." Dibrell said.

Preston didn't say anything—he just smiled.

CHAPTER FIFTEEN

Sin City, Texas: Easy on gamblers, tough on reporters

1955

In the early morning hours of Friday, Aug. 5, 1955, two journalists working for Life magazine hid in the shadows outside the Turf Athletic Club, a well-known Galveston gambling den owned by Vic and Anthony Fertitta. They were working on an article about the island's reputation as "the last sin city." A photo of the infamous club would be the perfect capstone to the story.

But the doorman spotted them, and thinking they might be robbers casing the joint, he alerted Anthony Fertitta. Once they realized they'd been "made," Henry Suydam, Life's Dallas bureau chief, and photographer Joe Scherschel, ran—with Fertitta not far behind. The journalists ducked into a nearby alley, scrambled into their waiting car—a green station wagon—and headed for the Hotel Galvez.

Scherschel went up to their room with the camera equipment. Fertitta caught up with Suydam in the lobby and demanded to know who he was. When the desk clerk identified the men as reporters, Fertitta slapped Suydam across the face.

"I am a member of the Greater Galveston Beach Association and for the past four years we have been asking Life to send reporters down here and cover some of our big events, but they never have," Suydam later recalled Fertitta telling him. "And now you come sneaking around."

Suydam said Fertitta told him he would have let the men take pictures, if they'd just asked. Then Fertitta apologized for hitting him, shook Suydam's hand, and gave him a $20 bill. He also tipped the desk clerk and the switchboard operator $5 each and apologized for causing a disturbance. When Suydam wouldn't take the money, Fertitta left it in an envelope for the hotel manager.

Later that day, Fertitta and his attorneys met with Galveston Mayor George Roy Clough, City Attorney James Phipps, the two Galvez employees who witnessed the incident, and the hotel's lawyers. On Saturday, Life's publisher, Andrew Heiskell, wired Clough, Phipps, District Attorney Marsene Johnson Jr., and Texas Gov. Allan Shivers to demand action about the interference with "the freedom of the press." Johnson wired back to say Suydam had left the island without filing a police report, the first step toward any type of prosecution.

The next day, newspapers across the state were filled with stories about the incident, not exactly the kind of press the Greater Galveston Beach Association wanted.

On Monday, flanked by his Houston attorney, Suydam came back to Galveston to file charges against Fertitta. Judge James L. McKenna held a hearing on the incident immediately. Fertitta didn't dispute what happened, although he said he didn't hit Suydam hard. McKenna found him guilty of simple assault and fined him $25.

After the verdict, Fertitta shook hands with Suydam and his lawyer. Apparently, there were no hard feelings, although that might not have remained true after Life published Suydam's story. The headline: "Wide-open Galveston mocks Texas laws."

Stolen whiskey shipment leads to downtown gunfight

1931

How many gunfights can be blamed on alcohol and bad blood? In most cases it only takes a few drinks too many to turn a good time into a murder investigation. But the shootout that sent downtown Galveston shoppers scrambling for cover in the spring of 1931—two years before the end of Prohibition—involved a bit more booze than that.

Several weeks earlier, three shipments of illegal Canadian whiskey belonging to a group of Galveston bootleggers got hijacked near Houston. It was the culmination of a longstanding rivalry between island and mainland liquor gangs. The island bootleggers reportedly issued an ultimatum to their Houston competition: the thefts would stop—or else. Intending to pre-empt an all-out war between the bootleggers, two men from the Houston gang came to Galveston to talk over the situation.

Clarence Gregory and Mitchell Frankovich, both of Houston, agreed to meet Theodore "Fatty" Owens and James "Jimmie" Crabb at Kid Backenstoe's news and cigar stand at 413 Tremont at about 3 p.m. on Friday, March 31. The four men talked for a while and seemed to have resolved the dispute amicably, according to witnesses. But as Gregory and Frankovich walked down the street, someone yelled, "Stick 'em up!" (No joke, at least according to The Galveston Daily News. Art evidently does imitate life.)

After that, the bullets started flying.

The four men, all clutching pistols, dodged between cars and into alleys, guns blazing. Shoppers scattered. Two policemen patrolling nearby heard the shots and came running. They arrived in time to see Gregory collapse in the street with a gunshot wound to his chest and one to his shoulder. The doctor who examined him later found two more bullet wounds. Frankovich, who had ducked down between two cars, also suffered a gunshot to the chest. The officers yelled for the shooting to stop, and it did, probably because the Houston men were incapacitated and not so much out of respect for law enforcement.

Bystanders quickly filled 23rd Street to witness the aftermath. Officers arrested Owen on the spot. While ambulance attendants scooped up Gregory and rushed him to the hospital, Frankovich staggered over and asked the police chief to take him to the hospital as well. Both men gave statements, implicating Owens and Crabb, who was arrested in a nearby restaurant about 30 minutes later. Police charged the men with attempted murder and released them on a $5,000 bond each. When Gregory died several hours later at John Sealy Hospital, Owens and Crabb turned themselves in at the police station to face murder charges. When he was arrested, Owens was carrying $1,000 in cash, worth about $15,654 today. Frankovich had about $700, worth nearly $11,000 today.

The next day, the men's attorney said they intended to claim self defense. But Frankovich told a very different story. According to Houston police, Frankovich appealed to them before the shooting for protection, claiming he feared for his life. They advised him to leave town. Instead, he went to Galveston. About a week after the shooting, not long after he got out of the hospital, Frankovich was charged with "rudely" displaying a gun and discharging it within city limits.

A Galveston judge eventually dismissed charges against Crabb, but Owens went to trial for murder in November. During the trial, several witnesses from Houston testified they heard Gregory threaten to kill Owens. Frankovich took the stand to claim Owens fired first and he only shot back in self defense. Although he denied being involved in bootlegging, he said he'd heard rumors that Owens had accused him of hijacking the whiskey trucks. He claimed he and Gregory brought guns with them to the island because they didn't want to take any "unnecessary chances."

When he took the stand, Owens told a similar account—with him as the hunted and scared victim. He said although he was not a bootlegger, he'd heard Gregory and Frankovich threatened to kill him. Owens testified he only pulled his gun and started shooting after the two Houston men followed him out onto the sidewalk outside Backenstoe's. He said he never aimed but just pointed the gun in front of him and pulled the trigger—as many times as he could.

Owens described himself as a legitimate businessman operating a hotel over the Martini theater, and several law enforcement officials, including the police chief, testified to his good character. Under oath, the chief admitted he and Owens had been friends for a while, and one of his officers admitted he'd been convicted of bootlegging himself before joining the force. But all of them said Frankovich had the reputation of being a very dangerous criminal, not to be trusted. (Owens clearly had the home-court advantage.)

But it didn't do him much good. After deliberating for 15 hours and 30 minutes, the jury returned a guilty verdict. They only gave him two years, so maybe his reputation as a "well-known Galveston character" helped after all. According to The Daily News, the verdict sent quite a "jolt" through the island racketeers because they thought Owens would have no trouble getting an acquittal. His attorney immediately asked for a new trial on account of "jury misconduct."

Judge Charles G. Dibrell denied the request for a new trial, upheld the verdict, and sentenced Owens to two years in the penitentiary on Nov. 19. But after the hearing, he called the verdict inconsistent because if jurors believed Frankovich's account of events, they should have given Owens a much harsher sentence. If, on the other hand, they believed Owens, he should have been set free.

The Daily News editorial board agreed with Dibrell's assessment about inconsistency but said that was the case in "about half" of capital trials.

"The American people have learned to be content with what they believe to be an approximation of justice, because in many cases they get so much less. ... But we do contend that the laxity of law enforcement in this county, throughout the entire process, tends to condone the palpable compromises juries often make in their groping after justice."

Headless, disfigured bodies confound island police

1988

In 1988, two grisly murders shocked Galvestonians and left them wondering whether they had a serial killer in their midst. Police did not believe the cases were connected and suggested the killers likely came from somewhere else. But residents remained nervous about the possibility the murderers would strike again.

As days dragged into weeks, and eventually months, with no arrests, islanders had to face the reality the killer never would be caught.

On April 1, 1988, a 16-year-old boy flying a kite at Galveston Island State Park spotted a woman's leg sticking out of a black trash bag hidden in some shrubbery. When police arrived, they discovered a body clad only in panties and a nightgown top—her head sliced off. The woman, estimated to be in her early 30s, also had been stabbed multiple times. Unable to locate her head, investigators took fingerprints from the body in hopes of identifying her.

The medical examiner wanted to send her fingertips to the FBI's lab in Washington, D.C., for printing and analysis, but fear over a new and terrifying disease derailed those plans. Federal officials refused to accept the fingers unless the medical examiner could prove the victim did not have AIDS. But the blood was too degraded to run an AIDS test, according to the medical examiner's office.

The agency eventually agreed to take the woman's fingerprints and enter them into the federal database, but they couldn't find a match.

Galveston police also couldn't match her to any missing persons reports, and no one came forward to claim her. Almost eight months later, investigators admitted defeat.

"In all probability, we're dealing with a victim who is not from here, who has been murdered in Galveston by someone who is not from here either," Police Chief Robert Steen told The Galveston Daily News. "God knows where they're from. We're dealing with an unknown, looking for an unknown."

Police never did discover the woman's identity—or find out who killed her.

Later that same year, on Labor Day, another young boy discovered the body of a woman behind the old K-Mart on Stewart Road. She was naked, and her face "was all burnt up," according to the 11-year-old boy who found her. Investigators later determined the woman had been strangled. After she was already dead, the killer put a gasoline-soaked cloth over her face and left shoulder and set it alight, likely in an attempt to conceal her identity.

The plan worked, at least for a while. Police brought in a forensic artist from Houston to do a sketch and distributed it to the media. But it would take months before they knew the woman's name.

Darlene Delany, 47, lived in Houston and was "a Bible-thumper who preached to the homeless," according to Galveston Police Lt. Rick Boyle. She was prone to disappear for long stretches of time, staying at shelters in Houston to live among the people she was trying to evangelize. Her children hadn't seen her in a while and noticed a resemblance in the picture of the dead woman from Galveston. But they didn't think anything of it until December, when she still hadn't come home. They contacted the police, who made a positive identification using fingerprints taken from one of her Bibles.

But that didn't get them any closer to figuring out what happened to her. A year later, the killer remained at large, and investigators had no leads in the case.

"We have no idea on a motive," Boyle admitted in 1989.

Twenty-seven years later, police turned to a new forensic science in a last-ditch effort to identify the first victim found in 1988. Phenotyping uses DNA to create a composite picture of what a victim might have looked like based on ancestry, eye, hair, and skin color, freckling, and face shape. The analysis determined the woman was of Asian descent, possibly from China. Galveston police distributed an image of what the woman might have looked like, but as of 2019, they still hadn't identified her—or come any closer to finding her killer.

CHAPTER EIGHTEEN

She shot him because she loved him

1950

On the evening of Sept. 27, 1950, Johnnie Louise Rogers had a couple of beers with a neighbor before going to the filling station where she worked—to get a gun. She put the .44-caliber Colt revolver in a paper bag and boarded a bus near her home on 83rd Street, heading into town. When she arrived at 911 33rd Street, less than a block north of Broadway, she stood on the sidewalk and yelled up through an open window for her lover.

Roy Hardy came to the door—but so did his wife.

"I told him, 'Roy, I've come to shoot you,'" Rogers later recalled. "No. I didn't mean it—I wouldn't have harmed a hair on his head."

According to Hardy's wife, Dolores, Rogers declared if she couldn't have the man, no one could. Then she pulled the trigger. Rogers later painted herself as the victim, saying she took a gun to confront Hardy because she feared what he would do when she tried to end things between them. By her account, the gun went off accidentally.

Passersby who rushed to the scene after hearing the shot found Hardy laid out on the porch with the two women tangled in a jealous catfight of slaps and scratching. When the ambulance arrived to take Hardy to the hospital, Rogers ran to his side.

"Oh, darling! I love you… I love you…" she cried as they wheeled him away.

The deadly love triangle began three years before, when Hardy walked into the Seabrook cafe where Rogers worked at the time. The divorced mother of three said she fell in love with the Galveston garage owner immediately. He told her he didn't love his wife but she refused to give him a divorce. He persuaded Rogers to live with him, and for the next three years they presented themselves as a married couple in Houston, Seabrook, and Galveston.

Dolores Hardy wan't unaware of her husband's dalliances. She told investigators she knew who Rogers was, knew "what" she was. The two women even met to talk about the man they both loved too much to give up.

"She was very determined to fight for Roy," Dolores later recalled. "She told me she was willing to fight to get him to the best of her ability."

Rogers admitted she loved Hardy intensely—"worshipped" him even. But she claimed by September 1950, she was ready to be free. She described him as a controlling, jealous man who refused to leave her alone, even though she told him she no longer wanted to live with him. She said he'd beaten her up twice already and she hoped taking the gun to his house would scare him.

Hardy clung to life at St. Mary's Infirmary for 11 days before he finally died. A Galveston grand jury indicted Rogers, then 29-years-old, for his murder. "The other woman," as newspaper accounts called her, pleaded not guilty.

During her trial, which started on May 21, 1951, witnesses corroborated Dolores Hardy's account of Rogers' intent to kill her longtime lover.

"I know you're going to die but I shot you because I love you!" Rogers allegedly told Hardy after shooting him, according to Robert N. Burns, who walked past the house shortly after the shot rang out. One of Rogers' coworkers also testified to hearing the woman say if she couldn't have Hardy, no one would. Until about three weeks before the murder, Hardy used to bring Rogers to work each morning.

Rogers supposedly told her coworker she finally figured out Hardy was never going to marry her.

On the second day of the trial, Rogers took the stand in her own defense, telling an emotional tale of love and desperation.

"I told him that as much as I love him—which I did!—I worshipped him!—I told him his place was with his wife and babies," she testified.

But she lived with Hardy for three years. They bought furniture together at Galveston's Star Furniture. Hardy bought her a car, and gave her a weekly allowance. Eleven women testified during the trial that the couple presented themselves as husband and wife.

When she finally met her rival, Rogers said she asked Hardy's wife why she couldn't make him happy so he would leave her alone. Rogers claimed Dolores said she didn't know why she couldn't make her husband love her. After several attempts to break things off with him, Rogers finally showed up at Hardy's door with the gun.

"I loved him! I didn't intend to do anything like that," Rogers said of the shooting.

The jury evidently believed her. After deliberating for about six hours, they reached a verdict at 3:30 a.m. on May 23, 1951. Although they found her guilty and imposed a five-year sentence, they recommended it be suspended. According to The Galveston Daily News, veteran lawyers said they'd never heard of a jury finding someone guilty of murder and recommending a suspended sentence.

Despite her unwillingness to divorce Hardy before his death, Dolores moved on rather quickly, remarrying before Rogers' trial even began. During her testimony, Rogers vowed she would love Hardy forever.

CHAPTER NINETEEN

Two stolen T-shirts nearly cost a police officer his life

1982

As dark settled in over the island on Jan. 21, 1982, Galveston police dispatch sent Officer Oscar Haynes to investigate a shoplifting report at Angelo's Gift Shop at 31st Street and Seawall Blvd. A man and a woman had stolen two T-shirts from the store before heading off to a nearby bar. Haynes arrested them both and put them in the back of his patrol car.

It seemed like a routine arrest.

But then Haynes decided to take the man out of the car to search him. Terry Lee Zokoloski, 19, later said he didn't plan to hurt the officer. He pulled his gun intending to startle Haynes so he could escape. He clutched the .38-caliber Colt revolver in both hands as Haynes spun him around. Then the gun went off with an explosive burst that sounded to witnesses like a car backfiring. The bullet struck Haynes in the stomach. As the officer fell to the ground, Zokoloski ran.

Doubled over at the back of his patrol car, Haynes managed to radio dispatch: "Officer down."

Paramedics rushed Haynes to John Sealy Hospital while his fellow officers began searching for Zokoloski. He hadn't gone far. They found him about 45 minutes after the shooting, hiding in a garage near 33rd Street and Ave. Q. Prosecutors charged him with attempted capital murder of a police officer. The woman, Tracy Ann Reed, described as Zokoloski's common-law wife, faced charges of shoplifting and misdemeanor theft.

David Smith, who graduated with Haynes from the police academy in 1980, said petty crime was much more common on the island in the 1970s and '80s, in part because of the booming tourism trade. Lots of visitors meant plenty of criminal mischief. But a police officer shooting, especially as part of such a petty crime, was unusual.

Haynes survived but spent a week in the hospital. He returned to the force three months later. On May 27, the city awarded him a Purple Heart.

Zokoloski went on trial June 23. Testimony lasted just one day. He took the stand in his own defense, calling the shooting an accident.

"I had thoughts of scaring him," he said of Haynes. "I didn't intend to shoot him. I just wanted to aim at him so I could walk away. I didn't want to shoot nobody. I felt bad after what happened. I wasn't expecting nothing like that to happen."

Zokoloski claimed he knew nothing about guns and ammunition and insisted he didn't know how the gun went off. He suggested his finger could have slipped onto the trigger or bumped the hammer. Defense attorney Charles Jordan argued for leniency.

"The state has shown there was an opportunity presented to this stupid kid to do something reckless," he said. "If he wanted to murder, he could have pulled that trigger five more times. He didn't do it because he did not intend to murder that police officer. He had the opportunity."

But after he shot Haynes, Zokoloski reloaded the gun as he fled. That indicated he intended to do more harm if he could, Assistant District Attorney Mike Guarino argued.

"If you want to send a message to the crooks that if they want to shoot a police officer they get one free shot, then acquit this defendant or convict him of aggravated assault," he said. "The evidence strongly suggests this defendant is guilty of attempted capital murder."

And that's exactly what the jury convicted him of.

During the sentencing phase, Zokoloski detailed a long list of trouble that began when he started smoking pot at age 11. He started doing speed and acid at 14. He dropped out of school in the eighth grade and spent time in four reform schools after getting arrested on burglary charges. Zokoloski's mother, Geraldine Farr, blamed his criminal bent on his lack of family life. He'd never known his father and entered the foster care system when he was 5.

Prosecutors asked for a life sentence. The defense argued for no more than 15 years. Judge Ed Harris settled on 30 years, handing down his sentence on July 7, 1982.

Haynes went on to serve out the rest of his career with the Galveston Police Department. He retired after 27 years and died in 2015. He was 61.

Smith, now executive director for the City of Galveston, remembered Haynes as a quiet guy who kept to himself but was well liked. He wasn't a "gung-ho" cop, and he had a reputation for giving suspects the benefit of the doubt, Smith said. That made his shooting all the more surprising.

Zokoloski served 26 years of his sentence, gaining parole on April 4, 2008. Police in Ohio arrested him in 2010 for failing to report to his parole officer.

CHAPTER TWENTY

Murdered over an insult

1966

Delia Smith wasn't the type of woman who hid in her house and avoided her neighbors. So when they went a whole day without seeing her, they began to worry.

Blanche Taylor stopped by to visit her 78-year-old friend in the early afternoon on March 28, 1966. Although Smith lived alone in her rented Texas City home, Taylor spotted a blue pickup truck in the driveway. Thinking Smith had company, Taylor walked to a neighbor's house and paid them a visit. As she left, she noticed Smith's driveway was empty. She walked around the side of the house and knocked on the back door.

When Smith didn't answer, Taylor called her friend's landlady. Nelda Simmons promised to go check on her tenant but got distracted and forgot. Smith's neighbors called again around 5 p.m. Beginning to share their alarm, Simmons took her neighbor, an off-duty Texas City patrolman, to check on the old woman. The house at 701 7th Ave. was locked, the blinds drawn. But they could hear the television playing inside. Simmons finally found a window leading to the back porch that had been left open. She crawled through into the back bedroom and crept down the hall to the kitchen.

Smith lay motionless on the floor, her clothes in disarray and a bloody dish rag hanging from her mouth. A 55-inch-long Venetian blind cord circled her neck three times, tied in a knot so tight it broke the skin. The tassel still dangled from the end. The right side of her face appeared bruised, as if someone had struck her with a fist. Her false teeth lay on the floor nearby. Texas City police found her purse on the bed in the front room, its contents dumped out on the bedspread.

Detectives spent about six weeks investigating the crime before finally arresting a 28-year-old construction worker and tugboat hand from Galveston. Police took Gus Luther Hammond into custody May 5. The next day, Hammond agreed to give hair samples and go to Texas Rangers headquarters in Houston to take a lie detector test. Less than 24 hours later, he'd signed two confessions.

Despite what seemed like a slam-dunk case, police and prosecutors released few details before the trial began Oct. 31. Stories in The Galveston Daily News held no hint of a motive and no details from the confessions. Attorneys went through 310 potential jurors before finally seating 11 men and one woman. They listened to four witnesses before the judge ordered them out of the courtroom to allow prosecutors and defense attorneys to argue about the admissibility of the statements Hammond gave investigators, confessions he said Texas Rangers beat out of him.

"I signed that statement because I didn't want to be beat up any more," he testified.

Hammond voluntarily went to the Texas City police station the day of his arrest after his sister, Edna Garess, turned away two officers who came looking for him. Hammond was staying with Garess at the time of the murder because he was separated from his wife, whose grandparents lived next door to the victim. Garess testified she thought the officers, who weren't in uniform, represented a finance company. When she realized they were with the police department, she woke Hammond at once.

Police said Hammond initially agreed to take a polygraph but when confronted with the machine said, "It's no use taking that test. I killed the old lady." On the stand, Hammond vehemently denied saying any such thing. He insisted he told officers he didn't know who killed

Smith, a position he maintained until two Texas Rangers began hitting him in the stomach. After that, he said he agreed to sign anything.

Judge L.D. Godard eventually dismissed Hammond's claim and allowed the trial to continue, with the confessions intact.

Hammond's attorneys called a long list of witnesses to prove Hammond could not have committed the murder. The coroner put Smith's time of death between 12:15 p.m. and 2:30 p.m. Hammond began the day by picking up his wife and stepson and driving them to Galveston to visit her parents. They arrived at about 9 a.m. and he left about 30 minutes later, returning at about 1:30 p.m.

A friend of Hammond's testified he came to the Surfside motel at about 10 a.m., looking for her husband. He stayed long enough to have a beer and left about thirty minutes later. Another woman testified Hammond came looking for her husband at about 11 a.m. but left after just a few minutes. One of Hammond's former employers testified he saw the family on their way back to Texas City, pulled over on Hwy. 146 between 1:30 p.m and 2 p.m. At first he thought their car had broken down, but Hammond said he just couldn't see in the rain. When he got back to his sister's house, Hammond had some dinner and went to bed. Garess testified she didn't notice anything different about him.

Defense attorneys tried to bolster Hammond's claims of innocence by noting detectives initially expected the suspect to be left-handed, based on the bruising on Smith's face. Hammond was right-handed. They also made much of the blue truck in Smith's driveway the day of the murder. Hammond didn't own a truck. The most interesting testimony came from Dee Jumper, a former neighbor of Smith's. Jumper claimed she found Smith badly beaten during the "winter holidays" of 1964. She said Smith told her on another occasion, "they've had me locked up for five days with nothing to eat," suggesting Smith had family members who might have harmed her. But defense attorneys didn't work beyond that to cast suspicion on anyone else.

Besides Hammond's confessions, police had evidence that placed him in Smith's house, even though he claimed he'd never been there. They found his fingerprints on her stove, and a forensic expert from the Houston Police Department's crime lab said hairs found on Smith's dress and sweater were similar to Hammond's. As for motive, police said he killed Smith out of anger over an alleged "insult" to his wife. Daily News reports didn't specify the nature of the insult. In his confession, Hammond said he tried to make the murder look like a rape and robbery to cover his tracks.

District Attorney Jules Damiani asked jurors to assess the death penalty. The jury began deliberating on Nov. 16, 1966, hashing it out for 4.5 hours before being sequestered for the night. They deliberated for another 5 hours and 20 minutes the next day before returning their verdict: Guilty. They fixed his sentence at life in prison.

When the foreman read the verdict, Hammond bowed his head and tears ran down his cheeks. His family sat in stunned silence before bursting into tears themselves. During the trial testimony, Hammond's wife, Jo, wasn't allowed in the courtroom because she was a witness. But every day she brought a clean shirt to her husband in the Galveston County Jail. After the courtroom emptied that final day, Jo sat outside the courthouse, watching pigeons play in the fountain.

Hammond initially planned to appeal but dropped the attempt in February 1967, saying he had no money to pay another attorney. He served no more than 13 years. In 1980, Hammond remarried and started a new life in north Texas. He died in 2007.

CHAPTER TWENTY ONE

Seaman's murder nearly sparks Israeli invasion

1984

Eliyahu Kedem left the cargo ship docked at Galveston's Pier 41 on June 20, 1984, and walked into town to buy gifts for his wife and two children. Despite the heat, the 41-year-old Israeli seaman refused to spend money on a taxi. He wanted to save the cash filling his pockets for his family. After making his purchases, he headed back to the 645-foot General Makleef, on which he served as the chief radio officer.

As he walked down 37th Street at about 10:30 p.m., a bag in each hand, he passed a group of men standing outside a lounge near Church Street. A few minutes later, two teens on bicycles rode past. Not long after that, a car drove by, its headlights illuminating a struggle near the train tracks just a block from Harborside Drive. In the yellow glow, the men standing outside the lounge saw three men struggling. One man fell to his knees and the other two hopped onto bicycles and rode back up 37th Street, carrying two bags.

The men watching thought they had just witnessed a robbery.

But Pete Kovacevich, the car's driver, realized it was much worse than that when he reached Kedem. The sailor, staggering near the train tracks, screamed hysterically as blood gushed down his face. Nearby, a foot-long 2×4 gleamed with fresh blood. Kovacevich called police, and two officers rushed Kedem to John Sealy Hospital. He died six hours later.

When Kedem's shipmates learned what had happened, they held a meeting to discuss what they should do. Someone suggested marching into the city armed with submachine guns. According to The Galveston Daily News, a local rabbi helped diffuse the tension by holding a service with the crew. Several members of Galveston's Jewish community also met with the men to explain how the U.S. justice system worked. Attorney David Jameson called Kedem's widow, Shalomith, in Rehovet, Israel, to give her updates on the investigation.

Two days after the attack, Galveston police arrested 18-year-old Emanuel Calvin Williams. A few days later, 19-year-old Ira Dean Stanley turned himself in. Prosecutors charged both men with capital murder, which carried a possible death sentence. They reduced the charge when the grand jury indicted the two men together, possibly because they knew it would be hard to get a conviction without definite proof of which man delivered the fatal blow.

Williams and Stanley pleaded not guilty.

The trial, before a 10-woman, two-man jury, began May 14, 1985. Medical examiner William McCormick testified Kedem suffered "torrential blood loss" from four or five blows to the head. Police believed robbery was the motive, noting the two bags Kedem carried had disappeared. But the attackers made off with much less than they could have: Kedem still had about $700 in his pockets when he arrived at the hospital.

On its second day, the trial unexpectedly ground to a halt when eyewitness Melvin Petteway refused to enter the courtroom.

"I was told I wouldn't have to testify, and I don't want to," he told District Judge Ed Harris.

Petteway, one of the men standing outside the lounge the night of the murder, said he was scared to testify. For hours he refused and declared he would go to jail rather than put his life at risk. Harris called in another lawyer to advise Petteway, who eventually agreed to testify. Despite the drama surrounding Petteway's testimony, the most detailed account of what happened that night came from Patrick Jones,

19, who testified he was standing outside the lounge with Petteway and another friend when Kedem walked past them.

Shortly after, Williams and Stanley rode past on their bicycles, Jones said. After the attack, Williams rode back by the lounge and went into his house nearby. He came back out to meet Stanley, holding a pair of shorts, and the two parted again, Jones testified.

Defense attorneys attacked Jones' credibility, claiming he just wanted to get his name in the newspaper. They asked why he didn't initially report what he saw to police.

"I didn't want to get involved," Jones said, later adding, "What you want me to do? Go down there? I witnessed a robbery. I didn't witness no murder."

Defense attorneys suggested the police at first thought Petteway and Jones might be involved in some way, but prosecutor Jim James insisted investigators never considered them suspects. While the witnesses might have had credibility problems, James faced a bigger challenge to his case. Petteway and Jones claimed to have witnessed the attack from four blocks away, a distance at which defense attorneys insisted they could not have seen what happened.

Lawyer G. Michael Cooper III urged Harris to allow the jury to have a "controlled viewing" of the scene, which would be better than having them go to the site themselves.

"The probabilities are that they will. You can't resist it," he said.

James said he would love for jurors to make the trip but feared an appeals court might find a trial error in such a stunt and reverse any future conviction. He called Cooper's request a "clever ploy" designed to free his client after the fact. Harris denied the request.

Investigators had other damning evidence, but no smoking gun. An FBI special agent testified blood found on the murder weapon and on Williams' bicycle came from a human, but she couldn't provide a more detailed analysis because the evidence had been "contaminated."

Stanley declined to testify, but Williams took the stand in his own defense. He said he and Stanley had ridden their bikes through the neighborhood the night of the murder but denied any involvement. They were going to a friend's house when they passed the lounge where the witnesses saw them, he said. When prosecutors showed him photos of the victim, Williams didn't flinch.

"It looks like a bad sight," he said. "I would hate to be in that position."

The jury sat through nine days of testimony but didn't need to deliberate long. They returned guilty verdicts after considering it for just two and a half hours. Stanley and Williams sat impassive as jury forewoman Flora Jones read the decision. Several members of their families began to cry. Jones later told Harris several jurors feared reprisals, a possibility he deemed unlikely.

After the conviction, Jameson called Kedem's widow to tell her the news. He also announced a fund for Shalomith and her two sons, 9-year-old Oded and 2-year-old Ofem.

"The killers are the ones who are responsible, but there's enough responsibility to be shared by the town," he said, adding whoever killed Kedem is "a Galvestonian who created orphans, and I don't like that."

A month after the trial ended, Harris sentenced Stanley and Williams to 60 years in prison. Williams earned parole on Feb. 24, 2010, and Stanley followed on March 9. They each served 25 years.

CHAPTER TWENTY TWO

Waiting forever to die

1980

On a balmy February day in 1980, Warren Eugene Bridge and Robert Costa holed up in their room at the Surf Motel in Galveston and drank. Sometime after dinner they ran out of beer. As the long night wore on, they hatched a plan to raid the Stop and Go convenience store at 710 Holiday Drive.

Bridge, who at 19 already had served prison time for three burglary convictions in Georgia, likely had no problem robbing the store. But when they got there, Costa pressed a .38-caliber revolver into his hand. Shortly after midnight, Costa walked up to the counter and asked for the beer, acting like he was going to pay. Bridge pulled the gun and trained it on the clerk, 62-year-old Walter Rose.

A few minutes later, two witnesses saw the men running from the store. When they went to check it out, they found Rose lying on the floor, four bullet holes riddling his body. An ambulance rushed Rose to John Sealy Hospital, and investigators began trying to piece together what had happened. In the store's parking lot, they found $24. The thieves had taken the cash from the register but dropped it in their rush to escape.

Back at the Surf Motel, Costa and Bridge told two friends what they'd done. They buried the gun on the beach and figured they'd gotten away with it. Bridge followed the investigation in The Galveston Daily News, clipping stories and stashing them in a small photo album. They included updates on Rose, still fighting for his life despite his injuries.

Ten days after the crime, on Feb. 20, police executed a drug raid on the motel. After only a month on the island, Bridge had already earned quite a reputation for cooking and selling speed. The narcotics team found Bridge's meth lab—and his photo album of newspaper clippings. It didn't take long for him to confess to shooting Rose.

Four days later, the clerk died, and the district attorney filed murder charges against Bridge.

In early June, a welder began making repairs to a catwalk at the Galveston County Jail. He left a door unlocked, and Bridge saw his chance to escape. He and two other inmates ran through the door and kicked a hole into the jail's outer brick wall, dropping several feet onto the roof below. Someone on the outside spotted them jumping to the ground, but by the time jailers got there, the inmates were long gone.

Police captured one man quickly, but Bridge and the other inmate managed to get across the causeway before roadblocks cut off their escape. Reports of a shoplifter at a convenience store at Texas and First Street in La Marque alerted police to their presence. Bridge's accomplice surrendered, but Bridge escaped into nearby fields. Helicopters from the Pasadena Police Department and a local petroleum company criss-crossed the area, spotlighting the fields in search of Bridge. As dawn neared, search crews decided to regroup. Galveston County Sheriff's Deputy Wayne Cook had filled out his last batch of paperwork shortly before 10 a.m. and was headed home when he spotted a man walking down Hwy. 146 near FM 1765. Bridge didn't put up a fight when Cook confronted him, and the deputy arrested him without incident.

Two months later, Bridge went on trial. It took a jury of nine men and three women just 80 minutes to declare him guilty. The Daily News didn't bother reporting on the testimony details, announcing Bridge's fate in a 200-word, bare-bones story. Five days later, the jury delivered the "swiftest death penalty verdict in Galveston County's history"—taking less than an hour to decide Bridge deserved to forfeit his life.

Costa, charged with aggravated robbery, got a 13-year sentence. He served less than half of it, gaining parole on Oct. 28, 1986. Thanks to the automatic appeals process, Bridge was still waiting for his execution date when his accomplice walked free.

Bridge's life of crime didn't end with his incarceration. In 1984, he helped make a bomb and toss it into another man's cell. The victim was African-American and the man prison officials accused of orchestrating the attack was a known member of the Aryan Brotherhood. In 1985, Bridge stabbed another inmate during a riot, earning himself a separate 10-year sentence.

The Texas Court of Criminal Appeals upheld Bridge's murder conviction in October 1986. The Galveston court set his execution date for July 1987. With a month to spare, the 5th U.S. Circuit Court of Appeals granted a stay while his new lawyer, Galveston attorney Anthony Griffin, pressed another appeal. Griffin argued Bridge's first legal team provided him inadequate representation.

A year later, Daily News reporter Joel Krikpatrick traveled to Huntsville to interview Bridge. The convicted killer called Texas' reliance on lethal injection "cowardly."

"I would rather be shot," he said. "I would rather die standing up. The way they do it now is a druggy way to die. I wouldn't want to be hanged or to ride on old sparky. Just a plain bullet is cleaner somehow."

Bridge told Kirkpatrick he regretted killing Rose but didn't show much remorse. He revealed Rose's widow had sent him a Bible, "like she wanted me to repent or something." But repentance seemed far from his mind. He declared his victim got a better deal because he died quickly and didn't know what was coming when he went to work that day.

"If I had a worst enemy, and wanted to punish him, I would put him on death row and let him wait forever to die, not knowing when it would happen, but being almost sure it would," Bridge said.

At the time of the interview, Bridge thought he had just two more months to live. But Griffin secured another stay, this time from the U.S. Supreme Court. Eighteen months later, the high court set aside Bridge's sentence, asking the 5th Circuit to review the case in light of a new ruling that said juries must consider a defendant's mental deficiencies when assessing criminal penalties. By the time word of the stay came down, Bridge had already had his final meal: fried fish and french fries.

But he had many more meals before him. It took another two years for the 5th Circuit to reinstate Bridge's death sentence. On Nov. 22, 1994, almost 15 years after killing Walter Rose, Bridge finally ran out of last chances. Strapped to the gurney in the execution chamber, he directed his final words to his step-father: "See ya."

CHAPTER TWENTY THREE

Galveston dairy romance sours into midday murder

1941

Consuelo Holland stood outside St. Mary's Cathedral clutching her pocketbook and the tattered remains of her dignity. She would later say she didn't expect to see her rival, Marie Gulotta, at the church that day. She had come to offer a novena, a focused prayer said for nine days in hopes of obtaining a special grace. For the last year, Consuelo had watched helplessly as Marie tore her happy life to shreds. She'd begged the younger woman several times to leave her husband alone. But Marie didn't seem to care about anyone but herself.

When Consuelo arrived at the church shortly before 1 p.m. on April 25, 1941, she immediately spotted Marie. Standing on the 21st Street sidewalk, the two women argued over Leon Holland for the last time.

"I told her she had broken up my home and had ruined my life, and she said she had something in her pocketbook that would make me leave her alone," Consuelo later said. "I thought she had a pistol in her pocketbook, and I got scared and pulled out my gun and fired one shot and the gun kept going off and the next thing I remember I was sitting in the police car."

Consuelo fired her .38-caliber pistol six times, continuing to shoot after Marie fell to the ground. She hit her four times—twice in the front and twice in the back. When she ran out of bullets, Consuelo walked north, the gun still in her hand.

Galveston Police Officer John Lynch was driving by and saw the two women talking. He stopped a little further down the street and got out of the car. That's when he heard the shots and turned to see Marie fall. He caught up with Consuelo outside the Martini Theater. She offered no objection when he guided her back to the scene, never becoming hysterical, or even excited.

"She wasn't happy or smiling but she was very cool," Lynch said.

Father O'Connell came out of the church and gave Marie her last rites as she lay dying on the sidewalk. She was still alive when they loaded her into a J. Levy & Bro. ambulance, but doctors at John Sealy Hospital pronounced dead not long after she arrived.

About an hour after the shooting, the district clerk's office got its afternoon mail delivery. Among the other letters was a divorce petition, filed by Leon Holland on the "customary" grounds of cruel treatment.

The Hollands met in Houston in 1937, when they were both 28. Consuelo had already been married and divorced and had two children, including an 11-year-old daughter, Gloria. The couple quickly agreed to marry but couldn't agree where. Consuelo wanted a church ceremony, but Leon wasn't Catholic. He was willing to go to the courthouse, but she couldn't bear that thought. Unable to agree on how to say their vows, the couple settled on a common-law arrangement. They lived as husband and wife, and no one knew they weren't legally married.

The legality of their relationship didn't seem to matter. The couple got along well together. Leon bought Consuelo a wedding ring and even started going to church with her. Neighbors said the family seemed happy. Gloria, 15 at the time of the shooting, said Leon was good to her and her mother. She called him daddy.

But that all changed when Leon met 27-year-old Marie Gulotta at the Galveston Star Dairy, where they both worked. Consuelo first caught them together at the end of 1939 when she and Gloria walked to the dairy and hid in the back seat of Leon's car. He left work and drove around, eventually returning to pick up Marie. She said he was just taking her home. Consuelo asked how long that had been going on, to which Marie replied, "You just open your eyes?"

"I told Leon I didn't like him taking Marie home," Consuelo said. "I had never had a quarrel with Leon about a woman before that time."

After that, Consuelo started going to the Hollywood beauty shop on 21st Street, not far from the dairy, to watch her husband and Marie. "I could see there was something between them because of the way they looked at eachother," she recalled.

She continued to watch them together, catching them "hugging and kissing" behind the dairy. On one occasion, she ran across the street to attack Marie and Leon hit her. After they got home she said he beat her up. On another occasion, Leon pushed her into a can of lye when she attacked them as they "hugged and kissed" at the dairy. She confronted Marie alone in early December 1940. She told Marie she'd spent the best years of her life with Leon and admonished her for breaking up another woman's home. She told Marie she couldn't eat or sleep and she was a nervous wreck.

"She spit in my face, and I gave her a good beating," Consuelo admitted.

Marie filed a threats complaint against Consuelo with Justice of the Peace James Piperl, who had known Marie for a number of years. He talked to all three to try to get to the bottom of the dispute. Marie at first claimed she'd never had anything to do with Leon. She was "badly beaten up" but refused to testify because she didn't want to put her job in jeopardy or involve her family. Without her testimony, Piperl told her the case couldn't be prosecuted. Piperl told Consuelo that if Marie was bothering her she should come to him about it. He told Leon he needed to make up his mind. Leon told him that Consuelo was his common-law wife and that he intended to stick with her and "not fool around with anyone else."

Consuelo later said Marie "swore on her crucifix" she would leave Leon alone. But if Consuelo left Piperl's office with hopes of regaining her happy life, she was sorely disappointed.

Despite telling Piperl he intended to go back to his family, Leon moved out. That Christmas Day, he didn't come home, didn't buy his family a Christmas dinner, and didn't get Consuelo or Gloria a present. Although he no longer offered her any financial support, Consuelo continued doing his laundry, perhaps hoping her continued devotion would win him back. One day not long after Christmas she went into his room to drop off his clothes and found a shiny new radio. The box said it came from the Galveston Piano Co. Consuelo called the shop, and the clerk told her Marie Gulotta had purchased it for $26 (the equivalent of $457 today). When she confronted Marie, asking what right she had to buy Leon such an extravagant gift, Marie told Consuelo she could do what she wanted with her own money.

While Leon enjoyed his girlfriend's expensive gifts, Consuelo was running out of money to buy food. Gloria recalled they were always hungry after Leon left. Consuelo pawned her furniture and clothes, as well as her daughter's watch and cross to get something to eat. Her neighbors helped her as much as they could, but she finally had to get a job as a waitress at the Rio Grande Cafe on west Market for $7 a week and eats. She continued to beg Leon to come home, appeals he often rejected with violence. On one occasion, he knocked her teeth out during a fight over their separation.

Two nights before the shooting, Leon found out Gloria was going out dancing with some other young people. He confronted her, slapping her around when she protested. Consuelo told him if he ever laid a hand on Gloria again, she would kill him and herself. The next day, she pawned a coat for $7 and bought the .38-caliber pistol. She later said Leon was "beating her more than she could stand," and she wanted something to protect herself. The owner of a local sporting goods store said she brought the gun into his shop and asked him what kind of bullets it needed. She bought six and asked him to show her how to load it.

While Consuelo contemplated self-defense, Marie was making her final move to separate Leon from his wife for good. She'd already given him between $250 and $300 ($4,400-$5,300 today) in small weekly deposits to a bank account she'd instructed him to open. She told him to take what would be the last installment to a lawyer and have him draw up the divorce filing.

When Consuelo confronted her on the sidewalk outside St. Mary's, Marie had the lawyer's receipt in her purse.

Consuelo Holland went on trial for murder on July 15, 1941.

During jury selection, attorney Henry Greenberg laid out a three-pronged defense: temporary insanity, self-defense, and defense of the sanctity of her home. Texas law at the time gave men wide latitude to defend their marriages against romantic intruders, with lethal force if necessary. Greenberg asked potential jurors whether they thought a wife had as much right as a husband to defend the sanctity of her home.

The first day of testimony drew throngs of spectators, mostly women, who listened intently to both Consuelo and Leon's testimony. After telling her story, Consuelo insisted she didn't intend to shoot Marie and didn't know she would see her the day of the murder. She also said she still loved her husband.

Leon admitted he'd become "infatuated" with Marie and thought he loved her more than his wife. He didn't deny beating Consuelo when she caught him with his mistress. He admitted having "relations" with Marie, although he couldn't recall how many times. He said he rarely took his wife out in his car after that but took Marie out maybe twice a week. Assistant County Attorney Emmett Magee accused him of trying to "blacken" the dead girl's memory by sharing explicit details of their relationship. Leon said he just wanted to tell the truth. He said he supposed if Marie hadn't had anything to do with him he would have remained happy with his wife.

He also said he had come to his senses and was in love with his wife again. He said he intended to go back to her if she'd have him.

Magee tried to cast doubt about Leon and Marie's relationship, calling two of the dead girl's 10 siblings to the stand to testify they had no idea she was seeing a married man. One of Marie's brothers disputed Leon's claim that he spent New Year's Day with Marie. He insisted the whole family spent the day together at their parents' house, to which Leon never would have been invited.

The prosecutor also raised questions about Consuelo's character, suggesting she wasn't as much of a victim as she wanted jurors to believe. On cross examination, he asked her whether she'd ever gone out with another man or gone into a house in the red light district. Consuelo denied it all, including "taking sailors upstairs" in a west Market Street beer joint. She insisted she'd been true to Leon.

During closing arguments, Magee argued Consuelo killed Marie in cold blood. He urged the jury to give a verdict based on the evidence, not on their sympathy for Consuelo.

"I ask you in almost solemn prayer to convict this woman," Magee said. "The law gives her no justification for this killing. A human life has been destroyed, and the person who destroyed that life should not be allowed to go unwhipped of justice."

Greenberg pleaded with jurors to consider what Consuelo had suffered, asking for a suspended sentence.

Jurors began deliberating at 5:30 p.m. and hadn't reached a verdict after six hours. That edition of The Galveston Daily News is missing from the archive, leaving the reaction to the verdict a mystery. The trial's outcome would be lost to history as well if not for a short notice, printed five days later, about the withdrawal of Leon Holland's divorce petition. That brief account noted the jury convicted Consuelo of murder without malice and gave her a five-year suspended sentence.

The Hollands left Galveston sometime after that. They are buried in Seaside Memorial Park in Corpus Christi. Consuelo died in 1973. Leon lived another 12 years, dying in 1985.

CHAPTER TWENTY FOUR

The little girl who beat the odds—and the tide

1980

Clouds hid the sun and a chilly breeze blew off the Gulf of Mexico when an 8-year-old Galveston girl asked her father if she could walk down to the beach in front of the seawall by herself.

These days, few parents would ever agree to such a request. But this was March 19, 1980. The world seemed like a much safer place.

The girl played happily on the seawall just west of 45th Street until a long-haired man with a backpack approached her. A Canadian tourist spotted the pair talking. Something about their interaction struck him as odd. But he didn't interfere.

When the girl didn't come home as darkness fell, her worried father called police. An off-duty officer and several medical technicians searched the area where she was last seen until about 4 a.m. Thursday, with no luck.

After the Canadian tourist learned the girl had gone missing, he reported what he'd seen. When the sun rose, he joined Galveston Police Officer Richard Singleton to search for her. As they picked their way over the rocks below the seawall at 46th Street, seagulls wheeled overhead, their plaintive cries piercing the chilly morning air.

Then the men heard another cry blending with the birds but resonating with pain and fear. It led them to a pile of rocks recently disturbed. Carefully they began picking up the boulders. Some weighed just a few pounds. Others weighed as much as 40 pounds.

Underneath the rocks, they found the little girl, battered and bruised. The rocks left severe indentations on her body and deep cuts on her arms and legs.

But she was alive.

They rushed her to John Sealy Hospital where doctors later reported her in guarded condition. Police said she hadn't been raped but might have been molested.

Based on the Canadian tourist's description of the man he saw talking to the girl, police picked up three men. They eventually charged Jeffrey Steven Goldberg, a 21-year-old drifter from California, with aggravated kidnapping and attempted murder. The charges could have put him behind bars for 99 years.

During a news conference held after Goldberg's arrest, Police Chief Ernest Galvan defended the department against criticism officers didn't act quickly enough. By the time darkness fell, it would have been impossible to find the girl, he said.

"We were afraid some men may have even stepped on the rocks where she was buried," he said, although he acknowledged the timing of her discovery was fortunate. "If she had been there any longer, you know what would have been the result."

Although The Galveston Daily News never named him, the Canadian tourist went home with a commendation from the Police Department for his assistance in the search.

Eight months later a Galveston jury deliberated only briefly before agreeing with both the defense lawyer and prosecutors: Goldberg was incompetent to stand trial and assist in his own defense. He ended up at a mental institution. He never stood trial for the attack: The Texas prison system had no record of Goldberg ending up in jail. And due to healthcare privacy laws it's impossible to tell how long he remained institutionalized or what happened to him if he ever got out.

By November, the newspaper reported the girl had recovered, at least physically.

CHAPTER TWENTY FIVE

Teacher's murder prompts death penalty debate

1993

Marionette Beyah moved to Galveston from Philadelphia in 1981 to escape a family tragedy. After the brutal murder of her mother and sister, she needed a fresh start. She didn't know anyone on the island, but she quickly settled into the community, becoming a passionate volunteer and a beloved college instructor.

When she wasn't teaching office technology at Galveston College, Beyah served at Market Street Baptist Church and at the Baptist Ministerial Alliance homeless shelter. In 1988, she met Gaylon George Walbey, a 14-year-old abandoned by his family after getting out of a juvenile detention facility. Beyah agreed to foster him, and he moved into her house in December. She wanted to adopt him, but his biological mother, Linda Alford, objected. Four months later, Beyah sent Walbey back to Child Protective Services (CPS).

Walbey had already endured a traumatic childhood. When he was 5 years old, his father kidnapped him. Alford was serving in the Coast Guard at the time, stationed in Florida. It took her five years to find her son, eventually tracking him down at an orphanage in Texas. How he got there wasn't clear. But her joy over their reunion evaporated after just a few days. He stole her car and tried to set fire to the family's home three times, succeeding once. He told her he heard voices and freely outlined his plans when she caught him plotting something bad. Those plans always included violence to family members, she said, but never threats against anyone else. A psychiatrist diagnosed him with schizophrenia and labeled him a "menace to society."

"He was a good child, but he was very ill," Alford later said. At the same time, she insisted everyone who met him fell in love with him. "He's such a special child, and people just feel it."

But Alford had come to fear her son. When he got out of juvenile detention, she refused to let him come home. She said CPS caseworkers didn't believe Walbey posed any danger. But Alford knew better.

"I was trying to prevent what just happened," she later told The Galveston Daily News. "I just wanted him to get treatment."

He spent the next five years in and out of mental institutions and group homes. In 1993, Beyah discovered Walbey, now 18, living on the streets.

"She called and asked me if I knew my son was out on the street with no place to go," Alford recalled. "I said, Ms. Beyah, my son is very sick and dangerous. You need to send him home right away."

It's not clear whether Beyah tried to convince Walbey to go back to his family. But the next time she saw him, it would be too late for persuasion.

On May 5, Beyah left Galveston College shortly after 5 p.m. to run home and change clothes. One of the buttons on her blouse had popped off, and she still had a test to give that night. She drove her new aqua and tan Ford Explorer a few blocks down Avenue O ½ and unlocked her front door.

Walbey stood in her living room, trying to unhook her stereo. Beyah started screaming, and Walbey "went into a panic." He grabbed a fire extinguisher. She ran but Walbey ran faster. He hit her repeatedly, smashing her head so hard that blood sprayed the walls and ceiling and dents pocked the heavy metal cylinder. She fought back, ripping off her false fingernails in the struggle.

"She fell and I stopped," Walbey later told police in a taped confession. "But she was still making noises so I started hitting her some more."

After that he grabbed a steak knife from the kitchen and stabbed her. The handle broke off, leaving the blade embedded in her back. She was still "making noises" so he grabbed a bigger knife and stabbed her again. "I tried to choke her with an extension cord, but it didn't work," he said.

When Beyah finally stopped moving, Walbey took her keys and drove off in her Explorer. He later told police he was thinking. Eventually, he came back to the house and covered her body with a blanket. Then he looted her stereo and VCR, returning a second and third time to get more stuff. Later that night he met up with a friend, who later described Walbey as "mellow" while they drove around in Beyah's car drinking beer and stopping to eat hamburgers and sell some crack.

When Beyah didn't show up for her morning class, which was scheduled to take a test, one of her colleagues went to check on her. She called the landlord, who called the police. Later that day, officers spotted Beyah's Explorer at the car wash at 59th and Avenue S. They found Walbey at the wheel and arrested him. He quickly confessed, offering a detailed description of the crime.

Prosecutors charged him with capital murder.

Three days later, Galveston College hosted an emotional public memorial for Beyah.

"The students loved her and she was an excellent teacher," said Dwight Courtney, Beyah's supervisor. "On her evaluation we would always get comments that we need more teachers like her."

Beyah's friend, Alfreda Houston, recalled her love for others, especially people in need: "Marionette felt she could change the world. That's the way she was. To know her was to be her friend. She was truly a spirit-driven person."

Walbey's murder trial began July 26, 1994. He pleaded not guilty, but defense attorney Jim DuCote didn't deny his client's guilt. During closing arguments he described the crime as opportunistic, not carefully plotted: "He was just trying to get himself out of a situation... He just lost his head." Prosecutors spent three days laying out the evidence against Walbey, and DuCote didn't present anything in his defense. District Attorney Mike Guarino told jurors the case "cried out for justice."

They evidently agreed, taking just 45 minutes to issue a guilty verdict.

During Walbey's sentencing hearing, several people pleaded for his life, citing his history with mental illness. A couple who ran a group home for abused children in Houston where Walbey spent several years, said he never showed any signs of violent behavior. His grandmother, Lola M. Phillips, testified Walbey used to tell her he heard voices telling him what to do.

"It's been very hard for me," she said. "I've been praying, asking the Lord for justice. That's my plea, to give him justice. But also I don't want him to die so young, but I do want justice."

The jury deliberated for about five hours before sentencing the 19-year-old to death. Before making the final decision, jurors asked to hear the taped confession again.

"From that, everybody was pretty well able to make up their mind," said jury foreman Donald Cobb. "There was a lack of remorse. And with the fact that there was no hard evidence to show mitigating circumstances, it was the only logical verdict in the end. ... The actions after the crime were certainly uppermost in my mind, and I think most of the jury agreed that was the real key to the final decision."

Walbey spent the next 15 years on death row. But in 2009, the 5th U.S. Circuit Court of Appeals ruled his trial attorney didn't properly investigate his horrific childhood and other mitigating factors. It overturned the death sentence and ordered the district court to hold a new punishment hearing. Kurt Sistrunk, who was the district attorney at the time of the ruling, announced his plan to pursue another death sentence in the case. But Jack Roady, who defeated Sistrunk in 2010, decided to drop the case after reviewing the evidence and talking to Beyah's family.

Walbey's death sentence became a life sentence in June 2011. Mental health advocates applauded the decision, arguing Walbey's long history with mental illness should prompt pity, not contempt. Heber Taylor, managing editor of The Galveston County Daily News, noted executing someone like Walbey would not act as a deterrent.

"If you're trying to send a message to other people who were raised in similar circumstances and who suffer from similar disorders, you have to wonder whether they could comprehend it. What message could a just society hope to send by executing someone like that?"

Walbey will be eligible for parole in May 2028. He will be 53 years old.

About the Author

Leigh Jones fell in love with Galveston while working as a reporter for The Galveston County Daily News. She's a Hurricane Ike survivor and co-authored a book about the island's recovery, Infinite Monster: Courage, Hope, and Resurrection in the Face of One of America's Largest Hurricanes.

Adventures took her out of Texas for a few years, but the island was never far from her heart. She started reading accounts of historic crime while researching ideas for a forthcoming mystery novel set in Galveston.

When she finally returned to Texas, she settled in the Houston area with her husband and daughter. They visit Galveston often.

www.ingramcontent.com/pod-product-compliance
Lightning Source LLC
Chambersburg PA
CBHW071213070526
44584CB00019B/3015